W9-BBV-942

GREAT TALES
FROM
ENGLISH
HISTORY

GREAT TALES
FROM
ENGLISH
HISTORY

Joan of Arc, the Princes in the Tower,
Bloody Mary, Oliver Cromwell,
Sir Isaac Newton, and More

ROBERT LACEY

LITTLE, BROWN AND COMPANY
NEW YORK   BOSTON

Little, Brown and Company
Time Warner Book Group
1271 Avenue of the Americas, New York, NY 10020
Visit our Web site at www.twbookmark.com

First published in Great Britain by Little, Brown and Company, 2004
First United States edition, June 2005

Library of Congress Cataloging-in-Publication Data

Lacey, Robert.
    Great tales from English history. Joan of Arc, the princes in the Tower, Bloody
Mary, Oliver Cromwell, Sir Isaac Newton, and more / Robert Lacey. — 1st U.S. ed.
    p. cm.
    "First published in Great Britain by Little, Brown and Company, 2004" — T.p. verso.
Includes bibliographical references and index.
    ISBN 0-316-10924-X
    1. Great Britain — History — Medieval period, 1066–1485 — Anecdotes.
2. Great Britain — History — Stuarts, 1603–1714 — Anecdotes. 3. Great
Britain — History — Tudors, 1485–1603 — Anecdotes. I. Title: Joan of Arc, the
princes in the Tower, Bloody Mary, Oliver Cromwell, Sir Isaac Newton, and more.
II. Title.

DA32.8L33   2005
941 — dc22   2004063351

10   9   8   7   6   5   4   3   2   1

Q-MB

Printed in the United States of America

FOR SCARLETT

CONTENTS

Map of England 1387–1688
(see map on page xii for battles)

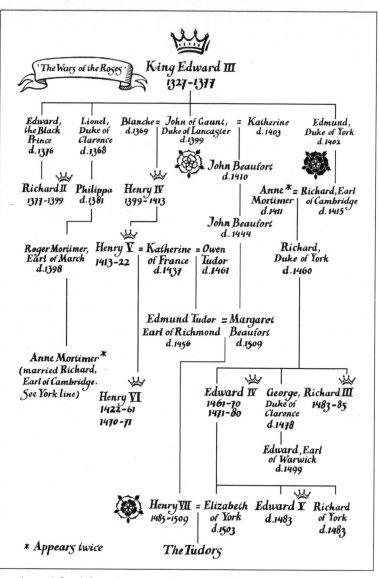

Simplified family tree, showing the Houses of York,
Lancaster and Tudor

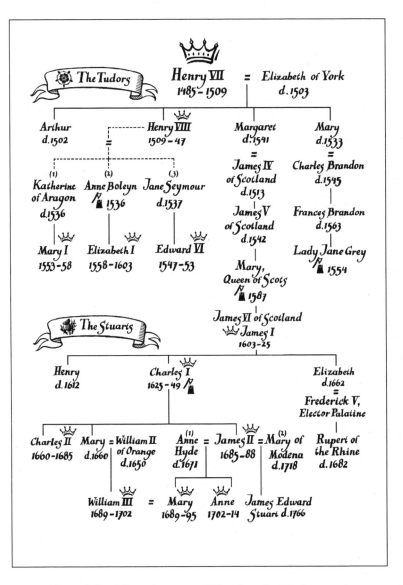

Simplified family tree of England's Tudor and
Stuart monarchs

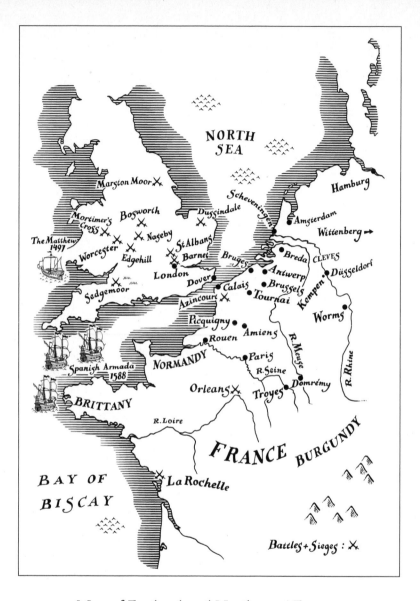

Map of England and North-west Europe
1387–1688

HISTORY IN OUR HEADS

FOR MOST OF US, THE HISTORY IN OUR HEADS is a colourful and chaotic kaleidoscope of images — Sir Walter Ralegh laying down his cloak in the puddle, Isaac Newton watching the apple fall, Geoffrey Chaucer setting off for Canterbury with his fellow pilgrims in the dappled medieval sunshine. We are not always sure if the stories embodied by these images are entirely true — or if, in some cases, they are true at all. But they contain a truth, and their narrative power is the secret of their survival over the centuries. You will find these images in the pages that follow — just as colourful as you remember, I hope, but also closer to the available facts, with the connections between them just a little less chaotic.

Our very first historians were storytellers — our best historians still are — and in many languages 'story' and 'history' remain the same word. Our brains are wired to make sense of the world through narrative — what came first and what came next — and once we know the sequence, we can start to work out the how and why. We peer down the kaleidoscope in order to enjoy the sparkling fragments, but as we turn it we also look for the reassuring discipline of pattern. We seek to make sense of the scanty remnants of the lives that preceded ours on the planet.

The lessons we derive from history inevitably resonate with our own code of values. When we go back to the past in search of heroes and heroines, we are looking for personalities to inspire and comfort us, to confirm our view of how things should be. That is why every generation needs to rewrite its history, and if you are a cynic you may conclude that a nation's history is simply its own deluded and self-serving view of its past.

Great Tales from English History is not cynical: it is written by an eternal optimist — albeit one who views the evidence with a sceptical eye. In these books I have endeavoured to do more than just retell the old stories; I have tried to test the accuracy of each tale against the latest research and historical thinking, and to set them in a sequence from which meaning can emerge.

The first volume of *Great Tales from English History* showed how the beginnings of English history were shaped and reshaped by invasion — Roman, Anglo-Saxon, Danish, Norman. And that was just the armies. The Venerable Bede, our first English historian, described the invasion of the new religion, which, in AD 597, so scared King Ethelbert of Kent that he insisted on meeting the Christian missionaries out of doors, lest he be trapped by their alien magic. We met Richard the Lionheart, England's French-speaking hero-king, who spent only six months living in England and adopted our Turkish-born patron saint, St George, while he was fighting the Crusades. Then, as now, we discovered, some of the things that most define England have come from abroad. Magna Carta was written in Latin, and Parliament, our national 'talking-place', derives its name from the French.

This volume opens in the aftermath of another invasion — by a black rat with an infected flea upon its back. In 1348 and in a succession of subsequent outbreaks, the Black Death wiped out nearly half of England's five million people. Could a society undergo a more ghastly trauma? Yet there were dividends from that disaster: a smaller workforce meant higher wages; fewer purchasers per acre brought property prices down. In 1381 the leaders of the so-called 'Peasants' Revolt' with which we concluded the earlier volume were men of a certain substance. They were taxpayers, the solid, middling folk who have been the backbone of all the profound revolutions of history. Later in this volume we will see their descendants enlisting in an army that would behead a king.

Changing economic circumstances have a way of shaping beliefs, and so it was in the fourteenth century. John Wycliffe told the survivors of plague-stricken England that they should seek a more direct relationship with their God, read His word in their own language, and not rely upon the priest. Wycliffe's persecuted followers, the Lollards, or 'mumblers', as they were called by their detractors, in derision of their privately mouthed prayers, would provide a persistent underground presence in the century and a half that followed. If invasion was the theme of the previous volume, dissent — spiritual, personal and, in due course, political — will take centre stage in the pages that follow.

Sir Walter Ralegh, one of the heroes of this volume —

and one of mine — is said to have given up writing his *History of the World* when he looked out of his cell in the Tower of London one day and saw two men arguing in the courtyard. Try as he might, he could not work out what they were quarrelling about: he could not hear them; could only see their angry gestures. So there and then he abandoned his ambitious historical enterprise, concluding that you can never establish the full truth about anything.

In this sobering realisation, Sir Walter was displaying unusual humility — both in himself and as a member of the historical fraternity: the things we do not know about history far outnumber those that we do. But the fragments that survive are precious and bright. They offer us glimpses of drama, humour, frustration, humanity, the banal and the extraordinary — the stuff of life. There are still a good few tales to tell . . .

GEOFFREY CHAUCER AND THE MOTHER TONGUE

1387

Whan that Aprill with his shoures soote
The droghte of March hath perced to the roote . . .

GEOFFREY CHAUCER'S *CANTERBURY TALES* opens on a green spring morning beside the River Thames, towards the end of the fourteenth century. Birds are singing, the sap is rising, and a group of travellers gathers in the Tabard Inn — one of the rambling wooden hostelries with stables and dormitory-like bedrooms round a courtyard, that clustered around the southern end of London Bridge. At first hearing, Chaucer's 'English' sounds foreign, but in its phrasing we can detect the rhythms and wording of our own speech, especially if we read it aloud, as people usually did six hundred years ago: 'Thanne longen folk to goon on pilgrimages . . .'

The pilgrimage was the package holiday of the Middle Ages, and Chaucer imagines a group of holidaymakers in search of country air, leisurely exercise and spiritual refreshment at England's premier tourist attraction, the tomb of St Thomas Becket at Canterbury: a brawny miller tootling on his bagpipes; a grey-eyed prioress daintily feeding titbits to her lapdogs; a poor knight whose chain mail has left smudgings of rust on his tunic. To read Geoffrey Chaucer is to be transported back in time, to feel the skin and clothes — and sometimes, even, to smell the leek- or onion-laden breath — of people as they went about their daily business in what we call the Middle Ages. For them, of course, it was 'now', one of the oldest words in the English language.

The host of the Tabard, the innkeeper Harry Bailey, suggests a story-telling competition to enliven the journey — free supper to the winner — and so we meet the poor knight, the dainty prioress and the miller, along with a merchant, a sea captain, a cook, and twenty other deeply believable characters plucked from the three or four million or so inhabitants of King Richard II's England. Chaucer includes himself as one of the pilgrims, offering to entertain the company with a rhyming tale of his own. But scarcely has he started when he is cut short by Harry the host:

> 'By God,' quod he, 'for pleynly, at a word,
> Thy drasty ryming is nat worth a toord!'

It is lines like these that have won Chaucer his fondly rude niche in the English folk memory. People's eyes light up at the mention of *The Canterbury Tales*, as they recall embarrassed schoolteachers struggling to explain words like 'turd' and to bypass tales of backsides being stuck out of windows. 'Please, sir, what is this "something" that is "rough and hairy"?'

In one passage Chaucer describes a friar (or religious brother, from the French word *frère*) who, while visiting hell in the course of a dream, is pleased to detect no trace of other friars, and complacently concludes that all friars must go to heaven.

'Oh *no*, we've got millions of them here!' an angel corrects him, pointing to the Devil's massively broad tail:

> 'Hold up thy tayl, thou Satanas!' quod he,
> 'Shewe forth thyn ers, and lat the frere se . . .'

Whereupon twenty thousand friars swarm out of the Devil's *ers* and fly around hell like angry bees, before creeping back inside their warm and cosy home for eternity.

In gathering for a pilgrimage, Chaucer's travellers were taking part in a Church-inspired ritual. But the poet's message was that the Church — the massive nationalised industry that ran the schools and hospitals of medieval England as well as its worship — was in serious trouble. While his imaginary company of pilgrims included a pious Oxford cleric and a parish priest who was a genuinely good shepherd to his flock, it also included men who were only too happy to make a corrupt living out of God's service on earth: a worldly monk who liked to feast on roast swan; a pimpled 'Summoner' who took bribes from sinners *not* to summon them to the church courts; and a 'Pardoner' who sold bogus relics like the veil of the Virgin Mary (actually an old pillowcase) and a rubble of pig's bones that he labelled as belonging to various saints. Buy one of these, was the message of this medieval insurance salesman, and you would go straight to heaven.

Chaucer humorously but unsparingly describes a country where almost everything is for sale. Four decades earlier England's population had been halved by the onslaught of the 'Black Death' — the bubonic plague that would return several more times before the end of the century — and the consequence of this appalling tragedy had been a sharp-elbowed economic scramble among the survivors. Wages had risen, plague-cleared land was going cheap. For a dozen years before he wrote *The Canterbury Tales* Chaucer had lived over the Aldgate, or 'Old Gate', the most easterly of the six gates in London's fortified wall, and from his windows in the arch he had been able to look down on the changing scene. In 1381 the angry men of Essex had come and gone through the Aldgate, waving their billhooks — the 'mad multitude' known to history as the ill-fated Peasants' Revolt. During the plague years the city's iron-wheeled refuse carts had rumbled beneath the poet's floorboards with their bouncing heaps of corpses, heading for the limepits.

Chaucer paints the keen detail of this reviving community in a newly revived language — the spoken English that the Norman Conquest had threatened to suppress. Written between 1387 and 1400, the year of Chaucer's death, *The Canterbury Tales* is one of the earliest pieces of English that is intelligible to a modern ear. For three hundred years English had endured among the ordinary people, and particularly among the gentry. Even in French-speaking noble households Anglo-Saxon wives and local nursemaids had chattered to children in the native language. English had survived because it was literally the mother tongue, and it was in these post-plague years that it reasserted itself. In 1356 the Mayor of London decreed that English should be the language of council meetings, and in 1363 the Lord Chancellor made a point of opening Parliament in English — not, as had previously been the case, in the language of the enemy across the Channel.

Geoffrey Chaucer's cheery and companionable writing sets out the ideas that are the themes of this volume. In the pages that follow we shall trace the unstoppable spread of the English language — carried from England in the course of the next few centuries to the far side of the world. We shall see men and women reject the commerce of the old religion, while making fortunes from the new. And as they change their views about God, they will also change their views profoundly about the authority of kings and earthly power. They will sharpen their words and start freeing their minds — and in embarking upon that, they will also begin the uncertain process of freeing themselves.

THE DEPOSING OF
KING RICHARD II

1399

THE LAST TIME WE MET RICHARD II HE WAS a boy of fourteen, facing down Wat Tyler and his rebels at the climax of the Peasants' Revolt. 'Sirs, will you shoot your king? I will be your captain!' the young man had cried in June 1381 as the 'mad multitude' massed angrily on the grass at Smithfield outside the city walls. His domineering uncle John of Gaunt was away from London, negotiating a truce in Scotland, and Richard's advisers had shown themselves wavering. But the boy king had said his prayers and ridden out to face the brandished billhooks.

An uncomplicated faith brought Richard II a brave and famous triumph, and it was small wonder that he should grow up with an exalted idea of himself and his powers. While waiting for vespers, the evening prayer, the young man who had been treated as a king from the age of ten liked to sit enthroned for hours, doing nothing much more than wearing his crown and 'speaking to no man'. People who entered his presence were expected to bow the knee and lower the eyes. While previous English kings had been content to be addressed as 'My Lord', now the titles of 'Highness' and 'Majesty' were demanded.

Richard came to believe that he was ordained of God. He had himself painted like Christ in Majesty, a golden icon glowing on his throne — the earliest surviving portrait that we have of any English king. When the King of Armenia came to the capital, Richard ordered that Westminster Abbey be opened in the middle of the night and proudly showed his visitor his crown, his sceptre and the other symbols of regality by the flicker of candlelight.

But Richard's public grandeur was a mask for insecurity. The King suffered from a stammer, and by the time he was fully grown, at nearly six feet tall, his fits of anger could be terrifying. Cheeks flushed, and shaking his yellow Plantagenet hair, on one occasion Richard drew his sword on a noble who dared to cross him, and struck another across the cheek. When Parliament was critical of his advisers, he declared that he 'would not even dismiss a scullion' from his kitchens at their request. When Parliament was compliant, he proclaimed proudly that he had no need of Lords or Commons, since the laws of England were 'in his mouth or his breast'.

Richard's dream was to rule without having to answer to

anyone, and to that end he made peace with France, calling a truce in the series of draining conflicts that we know as the Hundred Years War. No fighting meant no extra taxes, calculated Richard — and that meant he might never have to call Parliament again.

Some modern historians have frowned on Richard II's ambition to rule without Parliament. They condemn his attempts to interrupt the traditional story of England's march towards democracy — only six Parliaments met during his reign of twenty-two years. But it is by no means certain that Richard's subjects saw this as regrettable. On the contrary. The summoning of Parliament was invariably followed by the appearance of tax assessors in the towns and villages. So there was much to be said for a king who left his people in peace and who managed to 'live of his own' — without levying taxes.

Richard's gilded, image-dazzled style, however, won him few friends. He made no pretence to love the common man, and it was his attempt to 'live of his own' that brought about his downfall. When John of Gaunt died in 1399, aged fifty-eight, Richard could not resist the temptation to seize his uncle's lands. Gaunt's Duchy of Lancaster estates were the largest single landholding in England, and his son Henry Bolingbroke had recently been sent into exile, banished for ten years following a dispute with another nobleman.

Bolingbroke, named after the Lincolnshire castle where he was born in 1366, was the same age as Richard. The two cousins had grown up at court together, sharing the frightening experience of being inside the Tower of London at one stage of the Peasants' Revolt as the angry rebels had flocked outside the walls, yelling and hurling abuse. Some rioters who broke through managed to capture Henry, and he had been lucky to escape the fate of the Archbishop of Canterbury, who was dragged outside to be beaten, then beheaded.

Henry was not one jot less pious than his royal cousin. In 1390, aged twenty-four, he had been on crusade to fight alongside Germany's Teutonic Knights as they took Christianity to Lithuania, and in 1392 he travelled on a pilgrimage to Jerusalem. A tough character, the leading jouster of his generation, he was not the sort to surrender his family inheritance without a fight. Land was sacred to a medieval baron, and many magnates supported Bolingbroke's quarrel with the King. No one's estates were safe if the great Duchy of Lancaster could be seized at the royal whim.

When Richard decided to go campaigning against Irish rebels in the summer of 1399, his cousin grabbed his chance. Bolingbroke had spent his nine-month exile in France. Now he landed in Yorkshire, to be welcomed by the Earl of Northumberland and his son Henry 'Hotspur', the great warriors of the north. Henry had won control of most of central and eastern England, and was in a position to claim much more than his family's estate. Richard returned from Ireland to find himself facing a coup.

'Now I can see the end of my days coming,' the King mournfully declared as he stood on the ramparts of Flint Castle in north Wales early in August 1399, watching the advance of his cousin's army along the coast.

Captured, escorted to London and imprisoned in the Tower, Richard resisted three attempts to make him renounce in Henry's favour, until he was finally worn down — though he refused to hand the crown directly to his sup-planter. Instead, he defiantly placed the gold circlet on God's earth, symbolically resigning his sovereignty to his Maker.

Sent north to the gloomy fortress of Pontefract in York-shire, Richard survived only a few months. A Christmas ris-ing by his supporters made him too dangerous to keep alive. According to Shakespeare's play *Richard II*, the deposed monarch met his end heroically in a scuffle in which he killed two of his would-be assassins before being himself struck down. But the truth was less theatrical. The official story was that Richard went on hunger strike, so that the opening that led to his stomach gradually contracted. His supporters maintained that the gaolers deliberately deprived him of food. Either way, the thirty-three-year-old ex-monarch starved to death. According to one account, in his hunger he gnawed desperately at his own arm.

> *Of comfort no man speak . . .*
> *Let us sit upon the ground*
> *And tell sad stories of the death of kings!*

Writing two hundred years later, Shakespeare drew a simple moral from the tale of Richard II. Richard may have been a flawed character, but the deposition of an anointed monarch upset the ordained order of things. The playwright knew what would happen next — the generations of con-flict between the families of Richard and Henry that have come to be known as the 'Wars of the Roses'.

'TURN AGAIN,
DICK WHITTINGTON!'

1399

AS HENRY IV TOOK CONTROL OF HIS NEW kingdom at the end of 1399, he pointedly promised that, unlike his wilful predecessor, he would rule with the guidance of 'wise and discreet' persons. Richard II had been criticised for shunning the advice of his counsellors. He was nicknamed 'Richard the Redeless' — the 'uncounselled'. So Henry made sure that the advisers he summoned to his early council were a sober mixture of bishops and barons.

Then on 8 December that year the new King sent for a different sort of expert — a merchant and businessman, the first ever to sit on the Royal Council. Sir Richard Whittington was a cloth trader and moneylender from the City of

London, who had served as Mayor of the City and who would, in fact, be elected Mayor no less than three times.

'Oh yes he did! Oh no he didn't!' Every Christmas the adventures of Dick Whittington still inspire pantomime audiences in theatres and church halls around the country. We see Whittington, usually played by a pretty girl in tights, striding off from Gloucestershire to seek his fortune in London, only to leave soon afterwards, dispirited to discover that the streets are not paved with gold. But sitting down to rest with his cat, the only friend he has managed to make on his travels, Dick hears the bells of London pealing out behind him.

'Turn again, Dick Whittington,' they seem to be calling, 'thrice Lord Mayor of London!'

Reinvigorated, Dick returns to the city, where he gets a job in the house of Alderman Fitzwarren and falls in love with Fitzwarren's beautiful daughter, Alice. Disaster strikes when Dick is falsely accused of stealing a valuable necklace. So, deciding he had better make himself scarce, he and his cat stow away on one of the alderman's ships trading silks and satins with the Barbary Coast. There Puss wins favour with the local sultan by ridding his palace of rats, and Dick is rewarded with sackfuls of gold and jewels, which he bears home in triumph — more than enough to replace the necklace, which, it turns out, had been stolen by Puss's mortal enemy, King Rat. Alice and Dick are married, and Dick goes on to fulfil the bells' prophecy, becoming thrice Lord Mayor of London.

Much of this is true. Young Richard Whittington, a third son with no chance of an inheritance, did leave the village of

Pauntley in Gloucestershire sometime in the 1360s to seek his fortune in London. And there he was indeed apprenticed to one Sir Hugh Fitzwarren, a mercer who dealt in precious cloth, some of it imported from the land of the Berbers, the Barbary Coast of North Africa. Dick became a mercer himself (the word derives from the Latin *merx*, or wares, the same root that gives us 'merchant'). He supplied sumptuous cloth to both Richard II and Henry IV, providing two of Henry's daughters with cloth of gold for their wedding trousseaus. He also became a friendly bank manager to the royal family, extending generous overdrafts whenever they were strapped for cash. In the decades around 1400 Dick Whittington made no less than fifty-three loans to Richard and Henry, and also to Henry's son Henry V. He routinely took royal jewels as security, and on one occasion lost a necklace, whose value he had to repay.

Dick was elected mayor of London in 1397, 1406 and 1419. With the populist flair that a mayor needs to go down in history, he campaigned against watered beer, greedy brewers who overcharged, and the destruction of old walls and monuments. There was a 'green' touch to his removal from the Thames of illegal 'fish weirs', the standing traps of basketwork or netting that threatened fish stocks when their apertures were too small and trapped even the tiniest tiddlers.

Less kind to the river, perhaps, was the money that he left in his will for the building of 'Whittington's Longhouse'. This monster public lavatory contained 128 seats, half for men and half for women, in two very long rows with no partitions and no privacy. It overhung a gully near modern

Cannon Street that was flushed by the tide. Dying childless in 1423, Dick spread his vast fortune across a generous range of London almshouses, hospitals and charities.

The trouble is the cat. There is not the slightest evidence that Dick Whittington ever owned any pets, let alone a skilled ratter who might have won the favour of the Sultan of Barbary. Puss does not enter the story for another two hundred years, and was probably introduced into the plot by mummers in early pantomimes.

'To Southwark Fair,' wrote Samuel Pepys in his diary for 21 September 1668. 'Very dirty, and there saw the puppet show of Whittington which was pretty to see.'

Stories of clever cats are found in the earliest Egyptian and Hindu myths; Portuguese, Spanish and Italian fables tell of men whose fortunes are made by their cats. *Puss in Boots*, a rival pantomime, also celebrates the exploits of a trickster cat that magically enriches his impoverished master.

Experts call this a 'migratory myth'. Blending the cosy notion of a furry, four-legged partner with the story of the advancement of hard-nosed Richard Whittington, England's biggest moneylender, took the edge off people's envy at the rise of the merchant class in the years after the Black Death — these new magnates who mattered in the reign of King Money. And when it comes to our own day, Dick's tale of luck and ambition provides a timeless stereotype for the pop stars and celebrities who play him in panto: the classless, self-made wannabes who leave their life in the sticks and reinvent themselves in the big city.

HENRY IV AND HIS
EXTRA-VIRGIN OIL

1399

WHEN PARLIAMENT FIRST WELCOMED Henry IV as king in September 1399 with cries of 'Yes, Yes, Yes', he told them to shout it again. The first round of yeses had not been loud enough for him. At that moment the deposed Richard II, just a mile or so down-river in the Tower of London, was still alive. The new King quite understood, he told the company who assembled that day in Westminster, that some of them might have reservations.

This may have been a joke on Henry IV's part — he had a self-deprecating sense of humour. But the fact that he had usurped the throne was to be the theme of his reign. For his coronation in October, he introduced a new 'imperial' style of crown consisting of a circlet surmounted by arches that English kings and queens have worn ever since. He commissioned a book to emphasise the significance of England's coronation regalia — and he had himself anointed with an especially potent and prestigious oil that Richard II had located in his increasing obsession with majesty. The Virgin Mary herself, it was said, had given it to St Thomas Becket.

The fancy oil delivered its own verdict on the usurper — an infestation of headlice that afflicted Henry for months. He spent the first half of his reign fighting off challenges, particularly from the fractious Percy family of Northumberland who plotted against him in the north and were behind no less than three dangerous rebellions. In Wales the English King had to contend with the defiance of the charismatic Owain Glyndwr, who kept the red dragon fluttering from castles and misty Celtic mountain-tops.

Henry defeated his enemies in a run of brisk campaigns that confirmed his prowess as a military leader. But he was not able to enjoy his triumphs. In 1406, at the age of forty, the stocky and heavy-jowled monarch was struck down by a mystery illness that made it difficult for him to travel or to communicate verbally.

Modern doctors think that Henry must have suffered a series of strokes. For the rest of his reign he was disabled in both mind and body, though he went to great lengths to conceal his infirmity. Letters went out to the local sheriffs ordering the arrest of those who spread rumours of his sickness, while his bishops received letters requesting prayers to be said for his physical recovery. Depressed and speaking of himself as 'a sinful wretch', Henry came to believe that his salvation rested in a repeat of his youthful pilgrimage to Jerusalem.

One cause of his melancholy was the conflicts that arose with his eldest son, Henry of Monmouth. A brave and forceful warrior who fought alongside his father against the Percys and took charge of the campaign against Owain Glyndwr, 'Prince Hal' was not the dissolute hell-raiser portrayed by Shakespeare. But he was an impatient critic of the ailing King. In 1410 he elbowed aside Henry's advisers to take control of the Royal Council for a spell — it seems possible he was even pushing his father to abdicate.

In 1413 the old King collapsed while at prayer in Westminster Abbey. Carried to the abbot's quarters and placed on a straw mattress beside the fire, he fell into a deep sleep, with his crown placed, as was the medieval custom, on the pillow beside him. Thinking he had breathed his last, his attendants covered his face with a linen cloth, while the Prince of Wales picked up the crown and left the room.

Suddenly the King woke. As he sat up, the cloth fell from his face, and he demanded to know what had happened to the crown. Summoned to his father's bedside, the prince did not beat about the bush.

'Sir,' he said, 'to mine and all men's judgement, you seemed dead in this world. So I, as your next heir apparent, took that as mine own.'

'What right could you have to the crown,' retorted Henry wryly, 'when I have none?'

Richard's usurper never lost his sense of guilt — nor his

sense of humour. Looking round the room, the King asked where he was, and was told that he had been brought to the Jerusalem Chamber.

'Praise be to God,' he said, 'for it was foretold me long ago that I would die in Jerusalem.'

WE HAPPY FEW —
THE BATTLE OF AZINCOURT

1415

T HE NEW KING HENRY V WAS A TWENTY-
five-year-old in a hurry. He had been impatient with his
disabled father, and he was impatient with just about
everyone else. Watching a Lollard blacksmith suffering the
recently introduced penalty of being burned at the stake, he
had the man dragged out of the flames, then invited him to
recant. When the blacksmith refused, the prince thrust him
back on to the pyre.

Henry saw himself as God's soldier, and he had a soldier's
haircut to match: shaved back and sides with a dark-brown
pudding-basin of hair perched on top. This pallid young
warrior, with his large, fiercely bright, almond-shaped eyes,

brought intense religious conviction to England's long-running quarrel with France.

'My hope is in God,' he declared as he stood with his troops in the pouring rain on the night of Thursday 24 October, 1415. 'If my cause is just I shall prevail, whatever the size of my following.'

He was addressing his small, damp and beleaguered army outside the village of Agincourt in northern France. Here the English had been disconcerted to find their route back to Calais blocked by an immensely larger French army. Modern estimates put the English at 6000, facing as many as 20,000 or even 25,000. Henry's cause looked hopeless. A large number of his men were suffering from dysentery, the bloody diarrhoea that was a major hazard of pre-penicillin warfare. The French were so confident that night that they threw dice, wagering on the rich ransoms they would be extorting for the English nobility they would capture next day.

In contrast to the rowdy chatter and singing around the French campfires, there was silence in the English ranks, where Henry walked among his intimidated little army, doing his best to raise their morale.

'He made fine speeches everywhere,' wrote Jehan de Wavrin, a French knight who fought in the battle and collected eyewitness accounts of how Henry set about encouraging his men:

They should remember [the King said] that they were born of the realm of England where they had been brought up, and where their fathers, mothers, wives, and children were living; wherefore it became them to exert themselves that they might return thither with great joy and approval . . . And further he told them and explained how the French were boasting that they would cut off three fingers of the right hand of all the archers that should be taken prisoners, to the end that neither man nor horse should ever again be killed with their arrows.

Archers made up nearly four thousand of the English force — double the number of men-at-arms — and the English archers were crucial to what happened next day.

The French had chosen the ground on which they wished to fight — an open field, bordered by thick woods. But as their knights advanced in their heavy armour, the effect of the woods was to funnel them into the English bowmen's line of fire. The torrential rain the night before had turned the ground into mud, so the French slithered and stumbled, falling in their dozens beneath the fusillades of arrows. The white-feathered quills littered the battlefield, protruding from the bodies of both horses and men. It looked as if snow had fallen, according to one observer.

At the end of the encounter the English casualties were minimal, no more than two hundred. By contrast, more than seven thousand French lay dead, though many of their nobility died in circumstances their descendants would not forget. Under the pressure of a surprise counterattack, Henry ordered the summary execution of several hundred French noblemen who had surrendered but had not been disarmed. He considered them a threat. But in France to this day, the Battle of Azincourt — as the French call it — is remembered for this shaming betrayal of the traditional rules of chivalry. Modern visitors to the area are told that the battle saw the death not just of thousands of men, but of '*un certain idéal de combat*' — a foretaste of modern mass warfare.

For England, Agincourt has inspired quite a different national myth. London welcomed Henry home with drums, trumpets and tambourines and choirs of children dressed as angels. Flocks of birds were released into the air and gigantic carved effigies spelled out the meaning of the victory — a David defeating Goliath.

'We few, we happy few, we band of brothers', were the words with which Shakespeare would later enshrine Agincourt's model of bravery against the odds — the notion that the English actually do best when they are outnumbered. This phenomenon came to full flower in 1940 during the Battle of Britain, when Britain faced the might of Germany alone and Churchill spoke so movingly of the 'few'. To further fortify the bulldog spirit, the Ministry of Information financed the actor Laurence Olivier to film a Technicolor version of Agincourt as depicted in Shakespeare's *Henry V*. 'Dedicated to the Airborne Regiments', read a screen title in medieval script as the opening credits began to roll.

Henry V's own patriotism was deeply infused with religion. Dreaming of England and France unified beneath God, he had crusader ambitions similar to those of Richard the Lionheart, the warrior king he so resembled in charisma and ferocity. Like the Lionheart, Henry could not keep away from battle and, like him, he was struck down, young and unnecessarily, by a hazard of the battlefield when besieging a minor castle in France. Gangrene claimed Richard. Henry was felled by dysentery, contracted at the siege of Meaux. His boiled and flesh-free bones were borne back to England in a coffin topped with his effigy — a death mask of his head, face and upper body that had been moulded in steamed leather.

Just before he died Henry had called for charts of the harbours of Syria and Egypt, and was reading a history of the first Crusade. He was getting ready for his great expedition to Palestine. His wish to link England and France in this pious joint venture went beyond the simple jingoism of a modern soccer or rugby crowd. But one thing that modern fans might share with holy Henry is the two-fingered, 'Up yours' V-sign, directed derisively at the enemy. Possibly originating from the gesture presumed to have been made by fifteenth-century archers who wished to demonstrate that their bowstring fingers had not been cut off, it is known today as 'the Agincourt salute'.

JOAN OF ARC,
THE MAID OF ORLEANS

1429

JOAN OF ARC WAS THREE YEARS OLD WHEN Henry V won his famous victory in the mud of Azincourt. She was the daughter of a prosperous farmer whose solid stone-built house can still be seen in the village of Domrémy, near the River Meuse in Lorraine, France's eastern border country.

Today the border is with Germany. In 1415, it was with the independent and ambitious Duchy of Burgundy, whose territory stretched down from the prosperous Low Countries towards Switzerland. Joan's village was right in the path of the Burgundians when they came raiding, often in alliance with the English, as the two countries carved out conquests from the incompetently governed territories of France.

Henry V's famous victories, which continued after Agincourt, owed much to the weakness of France's rulers. The French king Charles VI suffered from long periods of madness, when he would run howling like a wolf down the corridors of his palaces. One of his fantasies was to believe himself made of glass and to suspect anyone who came too near of trying to push him over and shatter him. His son Charles, who bore the title of Dauphin, had a phobia about entering houses, believing they would fall down on him (as one once did in the town of La Rochelle).

The title of Dauphin, meaning literally 'dolphin', is the French equivalent of Prince of Wales, a title relating to the heir to the throne. England's heir had three feathers on his crest — the banner of France's sported a playful dolphin. But in the early 1400s the shifty and hesitant Dauphin of France did no credit to the bright and intuitive animal whose name he bore. The Dauphin's court was notorious throughout Europe for harbouring such undesirables as the paedophile Gilles de Rais — the model for the legendary Bluebeard — in whose castle were found the remains of more than fifty children.

France degenerated into civil war. King and Dauphin were at loggerheads, and England reaped the benefit in 1420 when the unstable Charles VI disinherited his equally unbalanced son. On 20 May, in the Treaty of Troyes, the French king took the humiliating step of appointing England's Henry V as 'regent and heir' to his kingdom, marrying his daughter Catherine to the English warrior monarch. So five years after

Agincourt, Henry V had within his grasp the glorious prospect of becoming the first ever King of both France and England — only to die just six weeks before his father-in-law, in August 1422, leaving his title to the long-dreamed-of double monarchy to his nine-month-old son.

It was three years later that the thirteen-year-old Joan first heard God talking to her in her home village of Dom-rémy.

'And came this voice,' she later remembered, 'about the hour of noon, in the summertime, in my father's garden . . . I heard the voice on the right-hand side, towards the church, and rarely do I hear it without a brightness. This brightness comes from the same side as the voice is heard. It is usually a great light.'

Anyone today who reported hearing voices would proba-bly be sent to a psychiatrist and might well be diagnosed as schizophrenic. But Joan had no doubt who was talking to her. 'After I had thrice heard this voice, I knew that it was the voice of an angel. This voice has always guided me well and I have always understood it clearly.'

The fascination of Joan's story is that a teenage girl should have persuaded ever-widening circles of people to agree with her. 'You are she,' said her angel, 'whom the King of Heaven has chosen to bring reparation to the kingdom.'

It was just what a divided and demoralised France needed to hear. After months of badgering, Joan finally won an au-dience with the Dauphin, and she galvanised the normally melancholic prince, who was now technically Charles VII but had so far lacked the push to get himself crowned.

Dressed in men's clothes, Joan had been led into court as a freak show. But the Dauphin was inspired. After hearing her, recalled one eyewitness, the would-be king 'appeared radiant'. He sent the girl to be cross-examined by a commission of learned clerics, and she confronted them with the same self-confidence.

'Do you believe in God?' asked one theologian.

'Yes,' she retorted, 'better than you.'

The practical proof of Joan's divine mandate came in the spring of 1429 when, aged seventeen, she joined the French army at the town of Orleans, which the English had been besieging for six months. Her timing was perfect — the English, weakened by illness, had been deserted by their Burgundian allies. Within ten days of Joan's arrival they had retreated.

What the English saw as a strategic withdrawal on their part, their opponents interpreted as a glorious victory inspired by 'La Pucelle' — 'the Maid', as the French now called her. Joan symbolised the purity that France had lost and was longing to regain. Her virginity was a curious source of pride to her fellow-soldiers, among whom she dressed and undressed with a remarkable lack of inhibition. Several later testified that they had seen her breasts 'which were beautiful', but found, to their surprise, that their 'carnal desires' were not aroused by the prospect.

Joan's voices had told her to dress as a soldier of God, and her appearance in a specially made suit of armour created a stirring image around which her legend could flourish. As her authority grew, she demanded that France's soldiers should give up swearing, go to church and refrain from loot-ing or harassing the civilians through whose towns and vil-lages they passed.

Volunteers stepped forward in their hundreds, inspired by the idea of joining an army with a saint at its head, while the demoralised English, once so confident that God was on their side, also began to believe the legend. When Joan was captured by Burgundian forces in May 1430, both the Bur-gundians and the English 'were much more excited than if they had captured five hundred fighting men', wrote the French chronicler de Monstrelet. 'They had never been so afraid of any captain or commander in war.'

The English promptly set up a church tribunal where Joan was condemned as a witch — her habit of wearing men's clothes was taken as particular proof of her damna-tion. If the Dauphin had exerted himself he might have negotiated her ransom, as was normal with high-profile prisoners-of-war. But he did nothing to help save the girl who had saved *him*. On 30 May 1431 Joan of Arc was led out into the marketplace in Rouen by English soldiers, tied to a stake and burned to death. She was nineteen years old.

'We are all ruined,' said one English witness, 'for a good and holy person was burned.'

Over the centuries England has chosen to remember the Hundred Years War for its great victories like Crécy and Agincourt: but, thanks to Joan of Arc, the bloody 116-year enterprise actually ended, for the English, in miserable de-feat. According to one account, a white dove was seen in the sky at the moment of the Maid's death, and the French took this to symbolise God's blessing. They felt inspired to campaign with even more righteous certainty, and by 1453 all that survived of England's once great French empire was the walled port of Calais.

Joan of Arc's scarcely credible adventure remains eternally compelling. The simplicity and purity of her faith have inspired writers and dramatists over the centuries — particularly in times when it has become fashionable not to believe in God.

A 'PROMPTER FOR LITTLE ONES'

1440

THE LONG LISTS OF LATIN WORDS IN GEOFFREY of Lynn's *Promptorium Parvulorum* would offer tedious reading for modern fans of Harry Potter, but his 'Prompter for Little Ones' has a good claim to being England's first child-friendly book.

Geoffrey was a friar from the Norfolk town known today as King's Lynn, and his 'Prompter' reads like the work of a kindly schoolmaster. It was a dictionary which set out the words that a good medieval pupil might be expected to know — many of them to do with religion. But defying the solemn tone, Geoffrey also listed the names of toys, games and children's playground pastimes. We read of rag dolls, four different types of spinning top, a child's bell; of games of shuttlecock, tennis and leapfrog, three running and chasing games, and games to be played on a swing or seesaw (which Geoffrey calls a 'totter', or 'merry totter').

All this gives us a rare glimpse into childhood in the Middle Ages. Medieval books were for grown-ups — most chronicles tell us of war and arguments over religion. But Geoffrey of Lynn takes us into the world of children, and shows us something of their preoccupations and imaginings.

In recent times this picture has been made real for us thanks to the chirps and bleepings of the modern metal detector. The Thames Mud Larks, named after the Victorian children who used to scavenge flotsam from the banks of the river, are a group of enthusiasts who scour the mudflats of the Thames at low tide. During London's construction boom of the 1980s they were also to be seen raking over the city's building sites, and what they came up with was an extraordinary treasure trove — large numbers of ancient toys.

One Mud Lark, Tony Pilson, retrieved hundreds of tiny pewter playthings dating back as early as AD 1250 — miniature jugs, pans, other kitchen and cooking utensils and even bird-cages. He and his fellow-searchers turned up just about everything you would need to equip a doll's house — along with small metal soldiers that included a knight in armour. Mounted on horseback, the little figure had been cast from a mould, so he must originally have been produced in bulk.

When we look at portraits of children in the Middle Ages, they usually stare out at us with formal and stern expressions. But in the pages of Geoffrey's 'Prompter for Little

Ones' and in the modern discoveries of the Mud Larks, we find evidence of so much infant fun and laughter. And since all these toys were made by adults, and must, for the most part, have been purchased and given as presents by parents and other fond relations, we can presume that medieval grown-ups recognised and cherished the magic world of childhood.

HOUSE OF LANCASTER:
THE TWO REIGNS OF HENRY VI

1422-61, 1470-1

HENRY VI WAS THE YOUNGEST EVER KING of England, succeeding his warrior father Henry V at the age of just nine months. When the little boy attended his first opening of Parliament, aged only three, it was hardly surprising that he 'shrieked and cried and sprang', as one report described.

The problem was that in the course of his fifty troubled years, this king never really grew up. Henry VI went from first to second childhood, according to one modern historian, 'without the usual interval'.

This is unfair. Henry was a kindly and pious man who financed the building of two gems of English architecture —

the soaring Perpendicular chapel of Eton College across the Thames from Windsor, and the chapel of King's College, Cambridge. He also ran a court of some magnificence, to which his naïvety brought a charming touch. The 'Royal Book' of court etiquette describes Henry and his French wife Margaret of Anjou waking up early one New Year's morning to receive their presents — then staying in bed to enjoy them.

But Henry showed a disastrous lack of interest in the kingly pursuits of chivalry and war. Faced with the need to command the English army in Normandy at the age of eighteen, three years after he had taken over personal control of government from his father's old councillors, his response was to send a cousin in his place. Henry felt he had quite enough to do supervising the foundation of Eton College. It was not surprising he developed a reputation for namby-pambiness. Riding one day through the Cripplegate in London's city walls, he was shocked to see a decaying section of a human body impaled on a stake above the archway — and was horrified when informed it was the severed quarter of a man who had been 'false to the King's majesty'. 'Take it away!' he cried. 'I will not have any Christian man so cruelly handled for my sake!'

Unfortunately for Henry, respect for human rights simply did not feature in the job description of a medieval king. Toughness was required. In the absence of a police force or army, a ruler depended on his network of nobles to ensure law and order, and if people lost confidence in the power of the Crown, it was to their local lord that they looked. They wore their lord's livery and badge — and it was these rival badges that would later give the conflicts of this period its famous name.

A memorable scene in Shakespeare's play *Henry VI, Part 1* depicts the nobility of England in a garden selecting roses, red or white, to signify their loyalty to the House of York or the House of Lancaster. It did not happen — Shakespeare invented the episode. 'The Wars of the Roses', the romantic title we use today for the succession of battles and dynastic changes that took place in England between 1453 and 1487, was also a later invention, coined by the nineteenth-century romantic novelist Sir Walter Scott. The Yorkists may have sported a rose on occasion, but there is no evidence that the Lancastrians ever did — at the Battle of Barnet in 1471, they started fighting each other because they did not recognise their own liveries. To judge from the profusion of badges and banners that were actually borne into battle during these years, men were fighting the wars of the swans, dogs, boars, bears, lions, stars, suns and daisies.

The struggle for power, money and land, however, certainly revolved around York and Lancaster, the two rival houses that developed from the numerous descendants of King Edward III (you can see the complications in the family tree on p. x). The Lancastrians traced their loyalties back to John of Gaunt, Duke of Lancaster, while the Yorkists rallied round the descendants of Gaunt's younger brother Edmund, Duke of York. Shakespeare dated the trouble from the moment that Gaunt's son Henry Bolingbroke deposed his cousin Richard II. But York and Lancaster would have stuck together under a firm and decisive king — and if Henry V had lived longer he would certainly have passed on a stronger throne. Even the bumbling Henry VI might have avoided trouble if, after years of diminishing mental competence, he had not finally gone mad.

According to one account, in August 1453 the King had 'a sudden fright' that sent him into a sort of coma, a sad echo of his grandfather, Charles VI — the French king who had howled like a wolf and imagined he was made of glass. After sixteen months Henry staged a recovery, but his breakdown had been the trigger for civil disorder, and in the confused sequence of intrigue and conflict that followed he was a helpless cipher. In February 1461 he was reported to have spent the second Battle of St Albans laughing and singing manically to himself, with no apparent awareness of the mayhem in full swing around him. It was hardly a surprise when, later that year, he was deposed, to be replaced by the handsome, strapping young Yorkist candidate, Edward IV (see p. 42).

In this change of regime the key figure was the mightiest of England's over-mighty subjects — Richard Neville, Earl of Warwick, who fought under the badge of the Bear and Ragged Staff. With no claim to the throne, but controlling vast estates with the ability to raise armies, the earl has gone down in history as 'Warwick the Kingmaker'. 'They have two rulers,' remarked a French observer of the English in these years, 'Warwick, and another whose name I have forgotten.'

When Warwick and Edward IV fell out in the late 1460s, the Kingmaker turned against his protégé, chasing him from the country. To replace him, Warwick brought back the deposed Henry VI who had spent the last six years in the Tower: the restored monarch was paraded around London in the spring of 1471. But the confused and shambling king had to be shepherded down Cheapside, his feet tied on to his horse. Never much of a parade-ground figure, he now made a sorry sight, dressed in a decidedly old and drab blue velvet gown that could not fail to prompt scorn — 'as though he had no more to change with'. This moth-eaten display, reported the chronicler John Warkworth, was 'more like a play than a showing of a prince to win men's hearts'.

It was the Kingmaker's last throw — and a losing one. Warwick was unable to beat off the challenge of Edward IV, now returned, who soon defeated and killed the earl in battle, regaining the crown for himself.

As for poor Henry, his fate was sealed. Two weeks later he was found dead in the Tower, and history has pointed the finger at his second-time supplanter, Edward. Henry probably *was* murdered — but there is a sad plausibility to the official explanation that the twice-reigning King, who inherited two kingdoms and lost them both, passed away out of 'pure displeasure and melancholy'.

THE HOUSE OF THEODORE

1432–85

IF THE WARS OF THE ROSES WERE FOUGHT BY the men, it was the women who eventually sorted out the mess. By the late 1400s the royal family tree had become a crazy spider's web of possible claimants to the throne, and it took female instinct to tease out the relevant strands from the tangle. The emotions of mothers and wives were to weave new patterns — and eventually they produced a most unlikely solution.

Owain ap Maredudd ap Tydwr was a silver-tongued Welsh gentleman who caught the eye of Henry V's widow, Catherine of France. He was a servant in her household in the 1420s — probably Clerk of her Wardrobe — and being

Welsh, he had no surname. The 'ap' in his name meant 'son of', so he was Owen, son of Meredith, son of Theodore.

But once he had captured the heart of the widowed Queen, Owen had needed a surname. According to later gossip, Catherine would spy on her energetic Welsh wardrobe clerk as he bathed naked in the Thames, and she decided she liked what she saw.

The court was outraged. An official inquiry was held. But Catherine stuck by her Owen and in 1432 their marriage was officially recognised. 'Theodore' became 'Tudor', and Owen went through life defiantly proud of the leap in fortune that he owed to love. Thirty years later, in 1461, cornered by his enemies after the Battle of Mortimer's Cross, he would go to the block with insouciance. 'That head shall lie on the stock,' he said jauntily, 'that was wont to lie on Queen Catherine's lap.'

From the outset, the Tudors confronted the world with attitude. Catherine and Owen had two sons, Edmund and Jasper, who were widely viewed as cuckoos in the royal nest. But the dowager Queen resolutely brought up her Welsh boys with her first-born royal son Henry VI, nine or ten years their senior, and the young King became fond of his boisterous half-brothers. In 1452 he raised them both to the peerage, giving Edmund the earldom of Richmond and making Jasper Earl of Pembroke. The two young Tudors were given precedence over all the earls in England, and Henry, who had produced no children, was rumoured to be considering making Edmund his heir. The new Earl of Richmond was granted a version of the royal arms to wear on his shield.

The Tudors rose still higher in the world a few years later, when Edmund married the twelve-year-old Lady Margaret Beaufort, who had her own claim to the throne. The great-granddaughter of John of Gaunt, she proved to be one of the most remarkable women of her time. Bright-eyed and bird-like, to judge from the portraits still to be seen in the several educational establishments she endowed, she was a woman of learning. She translated into English part of *The Imitation of Christ*, the early-fifteenth-century manual of contemplations in which the German monk Thomas of Kempen (Thomas à Kempis) taught how serenity comes through the judicious acceptance of life's problems. 'Trouble often compels a man to search his own heart: it reminds him he is an exile here, and he can put his trust in nothing in this world.'

Diminutive in stature, Lady Margaret was nonetheless strong in both mind and body. She was married, pregnant and widowed before the age of thirteen, when Edmund died of plague. In the care of his brother Jasper, Margaret gave birth to Edmund's son, Henry, in Jasper's castle at Pembroke in the bleak and windswept south-west corner of Wales. But some complication of the birth, probably to do with her youth or small frame, meant that she had no more children. For the rest of her life she devoted her energies to her son — 'my only worldly joy', as she lovingly described him — although circumstances kept them apart.

The young man's links to the succession through his mother — and less directly through his grandmother, the French queen Catherine — made England a dangerous place for Henry Tudor. He spent most of his upbringing in exile, much of it in the company of his uncle Jasper. At the age of

four he was separated from his mother, and he scarcely saw
her for twenty years.

But Lady Margaret never abandoned the cause. She would
later plot a marriage for her son that would make his claim
to the throne unassailable, and she had already arranged a
marriage for herself that would turn out to be the Tudor
trump card. In 1472 she married Thomas, Lord Stanley, a
landowner with large estates in Cheshire, Lancashire and
other parts of the north-west. The Stanleys were a wily family whose local empire-building typified the rivalries that
made up the disorderly jostlings of these years. Allied to
Lady Margaret, the Stanleys would prove crucial partners as
her son Henry Tudor jostled for the largest prize of all.

HOUSE OF YORK: EDWARD IV, MERCHANT KING

1461-70, 1471-83

THE FLAMBOYANT EDWARD IV SHARES WITH his luckless rival Henry VI the dubious distinction of being the only king of England to reign twice. In 1461 and 1471, thanks to Warwick the Kingmaker, the two men played box and cox in what turned out to be a humiliating royal timeshare. But after Edward had defeated Warwick and disposed of Henry, he ruled for a dozen prosperous and largely undisturbed years, during which he achieved another distinction. He was the first king for more than a century and a half who did not die in debt — in fact, he actually left his successor a little money in the kitty.

Edward was England's first and last businessman monarch. Clapping folk around the shoulders and cracking dirty jokes, he was also an unashamed wheeler-dealer. He set up his own trading business, making handsome profits on exporting wool and tin to Italy, while importing Mediterranean cargoes like wine, paper, sugar and oranges. He ran the Crown lands with the keen eye of a bailiff, and when it came to PR with the merchant community he was a master of corporate hospitality.

One day in 1482 Edward invited the Lord Mayor of London, the aldermen and 'a certain number of such head commoners as the mayor would assign' to join him in the royal forest at Waltham in Essex. There, in today's golf-course country, they were treated to a morning of sport, then conveyed 'to a strong and pleasant lodge made of green boughs and other pleasant things. Within which lodge were laid certain tables, whereat at once the said mayor and his company were set and served right plenteously with all manner of dainties . . . and especially of venison, both of red deer and of fallow.' After lunch the King took his guests hunting again, and a few days later sent their wives 'two harts and six bucks with a tun of Gascon Wine'.

It could be said that Edward IV invented the seductive flummery of the modern honours list when he made six London aldermen Knights of the Bath. Like the Order of the Garter, the Order of the Bath, which referred to the ritual cleansing that a squire underwent when he became a knight, was primarily a military honour. Now the King extended the bait to rich civilians that he wanted to keep on side: a moneylender would kneel down as Bill Bloggs, the sword would touch his shoulder, and he arose Sir William.

Edward understood that everyone had his price — himself included. In 1475 he had taken an army across the Channel where he met up with the French King at Picquigny near Amiens — and promptly did a deal to take his army home again. For a down payment of 75,000 crowns and a pension of 50,000 a year, he cheerfully sold off his birthright — England's claim to the French territories for which so many of his ancestors had fought so bloodily over the years.

The Treaty of Picquigny brought peace and prosperity to England, but not much honour. Edward's reign was too undramatic for Shakespeare to write a play about — one reason, perhaps, why Edward is sometimes called England's 'forgotten king'. But the beautiful St George's Chapel at Windsor, designed to outshine the chapel that his rival Henry VI had built at Eton College in the valley below, remains his memorial. And the Royal Book reveals a sumptuous court — along with a diverting little insight into how comfortably this fleshly monarch lived. After he had risen every morning, a yeoman was deputed to leap on to his bed and roll up and down so as to level out the lumps in the litter of bracken and straw that made up the royal mattress.

In 1483, Edward IV retired to his mattress unexpectedly, having caught a chill while fishing. He died some days later, aged only forty. Had this cynical yet able man lived just a few years longer, his elder son Edward, only twelve at the time of his death, might have been able to build on his legacy. As it was, young Edward and his younger brother soon found themselves inside the Tower of London, courtesy of their considerate uncle Richard.

WILLIAM CAXTON

1474

WARS AND ROSES . . . WE HAVE SEEN THAT roses were rare on the battle banners of fifteenth-century England. Let's now take a closer look at the 'wars' themselves. In the thirty-two years that history textbooks conventionally allot to the 'Wars of the Roses', there were long periods of peace. In fact, there were only thirteen weeks of actual fighting — and though the battles themselves were bitter and sometimes very bloody, mayhem and ravaging seldom ensued.

'It is a custom in England,' reported Philippe de Commynes, a shrewd French visitor to England in the 1470s, 'that the victors in battle kill nobody, especially none of the ordi-

nary soldiers.' In this curiously warless warfare, defeated noblemen could expect prompt and ruthless execution, but
'neither the country nor the people, nor the houses were
wasted, destroyed or demolished'. The rank and file returned home as soon as they could, to continue farming
their land.

In towns and cities people also got on with their lives.
Trade and business positively flourished, generating con-
tracts, ledgers and letters that called for a literate workforce —
and it was the 'grammar' schools that taught this emerging
class of office workers the practical mechanics of English
and Latin. The grammar schools multiplied in the fifteenth
century, and the demand for accessible low-price books that
they helped generate was met by an invention that was to
prove infinitely more important than considerations of who
was nudging whom off the throne.

In 1469 William Caxton, an English merchant living in
the prosperous Flemish trading town of Bruges, was finishing a book that he had researched. Caxton was a trader in
rich cloths — a mercer like Richard Whittington — and
books were his passion. He collected rare books, and he
wrote for his own pleasure, scratching out the text laboriously with a quill on to parchment. The book he was currently completing was a history of the ancient Greek city of
Troy, and the mercer, who was approaching his fiftieth birthday, was feeling weary. 'My pen is worn, mine hand heavy,
my eye even dimmed,' he wrote. The prospect of copying
out more versions of the manuscript for the friends who had
expressed an interest was too much to contemplate. So Caxton decided to see what he could discover about the craft of

printing, which had been pioneered by Johann Gutenberg in the 1440s in the Rhine Valley.

Travelling south-east from Bruges, he arrived on the Rhine nearly thirty years after Gutenberg had started work there. And having 'practised and learned' the technique for himself, the mercer turned printer went back to Bruges to set up his own press. In 1474 his *History of Troy* became the first book to be printed in English, and two years later he brought his press to England, setting up shop near the Chapter House, in the precinct of Westminster Abbey, where Parliament met.

Caxton had an eye for a good location. Along the route between the Palace of Westminster and the Chapter House shuttled lawyers, churchmen, courtiers, MPs — the book-buying elite of England. The former cloth trader also had an eye for a bestseller. The second book he printed was about chess, *The Game and Play of the Chesse*. Then came in fairly quick succession a French–English dictionary, a translation of Aesop's fables, several popular romances, Malory's tale of Camelot in the *Morte D'Arthur*, some school textbooks, a history of England, an encyclopaedia entitled *The Myrrour of the Worlde*, and Chaucer's bawdy evergreen, *The Canterbury Tales*.

More than five hundred years later a copy of Caxton's first edition of Chaucer became the most expensive book ever sold — knocked down at auction for £4.6 million. But in the fifteenth century the obvious appeal of the newly printed books lay in their value for money. Books became so commonplace that snobs sometimes employed scribes to copy Caxton's printed editions back into manuscript — while both Church and government became alarmed at the access to new ideas that the printing press offered to a widening public.

Over the centuries Caxton's innovation would marvellously stimulate diversity in thinking, but in one important respect its impact was to standardise. Caxton loved to write personal prefaces to his publications, explaining the background of the new book he was sharing with his readers, and in one of these he describes the difficulties of being England's first mass publisher. He was in his study, he relates, feeling rather bereft, looking for a new project to get his teeth into, and happened to pick up the recently published French version of Virgil's *Aeneid*. The editor in him couldn't resist trying to translate the great epic poem into English. Taking a pen, he wrote out a page or two. But when he came to read through what he had written, he had to wonder whether his customers in different corners of England would be able to understand it, since 'common English that is spoken in one shire varies from another'.

To make the point he recounted the tale of a group of English merchants who, when their ship was becalmed at the mouth of the Thames, decided to go ashore in search of a good breakfast. One of them asked for some 'eggys', to be told by the Kentish wife that she did not understand French. Since the merchant himself only spoke and understood English, he started to get angry, until one of his companions said he would like some 'eyren' — and the woman promptly reached for the egg basket.

'Loo,' exclaimed Caxton, 'what sholde a man in thyse dayes now wryte — egges or eyren?'

Even in this account you may notice that Caxton himself

first spelled the word 'eggys', then 'egges' a few lines later. As the printer-publisher produced more and more books — and when he died in 1491 he was on the point of printing his hundredth — he made his own decisions about how words should be spelled. His choices tended to reflect the language of the south-east of England, with which he was familiar — he was proud to come from Kent, 'where I doubt not is spoken as broad and rude English as is in any place of England'.

Many of Caxton's spelling decisions and those of the printers who came after him were quite arbitrary. As they matched letters to sounds they followed no particular rules, and we live with the consequences to this day. So if you have ever wondered why a bandage is 'wound' around a 'wound', why 'cough' rhymes with 'off' while 'bough' rhymes with 'cow', and why you might shed a 'tear' after seeing a 'tear' in your best dress or trousers, you have William Caxton to thank for the confusion.

WHODUNIT? THE PRINCES IN THE TOWER

1483

WHEN EDWARD IV DIED EARLY IN APRIL 1483, his elder son Edward was in Ludlow on the Welsh border, carrying out his duties as Prince of Wales. The twelve-year-old was duly proclaimed King Edward V, and leisurely arrangements were made for him to travel to London for his coronation. But on the 30th of that month, with little more than a day's riding to go, the royal party was intercepted by the King's uncle, Richard, Duke of Gloucester, at Stony Stratford on the outskirts of modern-day Milton Keynes.

The thirty-year-old Richard was the energetic and ambitious younger brother of Edward IV. He had been ruling the north of England with firm efficiency, and he claimed to have uncovered a conspiracy to seize control of the new King. He took charge of his nephew and escorted him back to London where, after a spell in the bishop's palace, the young Edward V was dispatched for safekeeping into the royal apartments in the Tower. There the boy was joined on 16 June by his nine-year-old brother, Prince Richard of York.

But only ten days later, claiming that the two boys were illegitimate, Uncle Richard proclaimed himself King. It was an outlandish charge, but he was formally crowned King Richard III on 6 July 1483, and the children were never seen at liberty again. With a poignant report in the Great Chronicle of London that they were glimpsed that summer 'shooting and playing in the garden of the Tower', the young Edward V and his brother vanished from history.

Few people at the time doubted that the King had disposed of them. But there was no solid evidence of foul play until, nearly two centuries later, workmen digging at the bottom of a staircase in the Tower of London discovered a wooden chest containing the skeletons of two children. The taller child was lying on his back, with the smaller one face down on top of him. 'They were small bones of lads . . .' wrote one eyewitness, 'and there were pieces of rag and velvet about them.'

The reigning monarch of the time, Charles II, ordered an inquiry. All agreed that the skeletons must be those of the boy king Edward V and his younger brother, murdered in 1483 by their wicked uncle. In 1678 the remains were ceremonially reburied in Westminster Abbey, with full dignity, in an urn beneath a black-and-white marble altar.

But over the years historians and physicians queried the authenticity of the bones. Did they really belong to the so-called 'Princes in the Tower'? And even if they did, what proof was there that they were murdered by anybody, let alone by their uncle? By 1933 the controversy was such that King George V, grandfather of the present Queen, authorised the opening of the tomb.

The two medical experts who examined the contents came to the conclusion that the remains of the young skeletons were almost certainly those of Richard III's nephews. Both indicated a slender build, with very small finger bones. Dental evidence set the age of one at eleven to thirteen years old, the smaller at between nine and eleven. Professor W. Wright, a dental surgeon who was president of the Anatomical Society of Great Britain, declared that the structure of the jaws and other bones in both skeletons established a family link, and he further suggested that a red mark on the facial bones of the elder child was a bloodstain caused by suffocation.

The notion of the victims having been suffocated made a neat connection with the first detailed account of the boys' deaths by Sir Thomas More back in 1514. Writing thirty years after the event, More pieced his story together through first-hand research — plus a certain amount of what he honestly described as 'divining upon conjectures'. Acting on Richard's orders, he alleged, two men had crept into the princes' bedchamber about midnight, 'and suddenly lapped them up among the clothes, so bewrapped them and entangled them, keeping down by force the feather bed and pillows hard into their mouths, that within a while, smothered

and stifled, their breath failing, they gave up to God their innocent souls'. More went on to describe how the murderers
then buried the bodies 'at the stair foot, meetly deep under
the ground, under a great heap of stones'.

We shall meet Thomas More again in a later chapter. His
name has become a byword for both learning and courage in
standing up for principle, and his unpublished account was
written at the behest of no particular patron. While clearly
disapproving of Richard III, he nonetheless made several attempts in his story to separate fact from rumour. But his research was seized on by others for commercial and political
reasons — most notably by William Shakespeare, whose
Tragedy of King Richard III, first performed in 1597, gave birth
to one of the most exquisitely chilling villains of English
drama: 'Conscience is but a word that cowards use . . .'

In Shakespeare's play we see the King ruthlessly order the
murder of his two nephews, along with the deaths of a
whole catalogue of other rivals and opponents — actually
uttering at one point the immortal words 'Off with his
head!' The evil that festers in the usurper's mind is graphically symbolised by his twisted and deformed body, reflecting sixteenth-century superstitions that Richard spent a full
two years in his mother's womb, before emerging with teeth
fully developed, a mane of black hair and a hideously
hunched back.

In reality, King Richard III was lean and athletic. His
portraits show quite a handsome-looking man, who may
possibly have carried one shoulder a little higher than the
other but who was certainly not the crookback of legend. Modern X-rays show that the higher shoulder in

one portrait was painted in afterwards. He was a devout Christian — something of a Puritan. He was an efficient administrator. And while he was certainly ruthless in sweeping aside those who stood in his path to the throne — including his helpless nephews — he was not the hissing psychopath of Shakespeare's depiction. The popular image of 'Crookback Dick' is quite certainly a defamation — one of history's most successful hatchet jobs — and it is not surprising that over the centuries people have come to Richard's defence. Founded in 1924, the Fellowship of the White Boar, now known as the Richard III Society, has become the most thriving historical club in the entire English-speaking world, with branches in Britain and North America.

In a testament to the English sense of fair play, the Ricardians, as they call themselves, campaign tirelessly to rescue their hero's reputation, and central to their argument is the absence of solid evidence linking Richard III directly to the disappearance of his nephews. More himself wrote, for example, that, having initially been buried beneath the staircase in the Tower, the princes' bodies were later dug up and reburied some distance away. So, argue the Ricardians, the skeletons discovered in the 1670s could not possibly have been the princes — who might even have escaped from the Tower.

As for the 'experts' of 1933, their techniques do not stand modern forensic scrutiny. To take one instance, there is no possibility that a single stain on an ancient bone could be plausibly linked to suffocation. In 1984 no less than four hours of television were devoted to a court-room inquest and trial in which this evidence and much more was minutely dissected and argued over by prominent lawyers and historians. Did Richard III murder the Princes in the Tower? The jury reached a verdict of 'not guilty'.

The debate will doubtless go on for ever — or, at least, until some conclusive new evidence is discovered. Modern DNA analysis could determine, for example, whether or not the bones that have lain in Westminster Abbey since 1678 are genetically linked to those of the boys' father, Edward IV, lying for over five centuries in his tomb at Windsor — though that would not tell us who disposed of the children.

Richard III's contemporaries had little doubt: 'There was much whispering among the people,' recorded the Great Chronicle, 'that the king had put the children of King Edward to death.'

'I saw men burst into tears when mention was made of [the boy king] after his removal from men's sight,' wrote the Italian traveller, Dominic Mancini, 'and already there was suspicion that he had been done away with.'

Medieval folk were not surprised by skulduggery and death at the top. In the previous two centuries England had seen three kings deposed (Edward II, Richard II, Henry VI), and all were subsequently disposed of in sinister circumstances. But to eliminate children — and your own brother's children — went one big step beyond that. Even if the physical evidence to convict Richard III of murder was missing, he was guilty of appalling neglect, for he had had a duty of care to his nephews. When it came to explaining what had happened to them, he never even tried to offer a cover story.

In any case, history's debate over the 'Princes in the Tower' lets Richard off too lightly. The younger boy was indeed a prince, but the elder one, Edward V, was a properly pro-claimed and fully acknowledged king, until his uncle went riding out to meet him at Stony Stratford on that late spring day in 1483. Richard might wriggle off the hook of modern TV justice. But he was found guilty in the court of his own times, and he was soon made to pay the full penalty.

THE CAT AND THE RAT

1484

EUROPE WAS SCANDALISED BY RICHARD III'S seizure of power. 'See what has happened in England since the death of King Edward,' declared Guillaume de Rochefort, the Chancellor of France, to the Estates-General, France's Parliament, in a speech that positively oozed gloating disapproval. 'His children, already big and courageous, have been slaughtered with impunity, and their murderer, with the support of the people, has received the crown.'

In fact, the support of England's people for their self-appointed monarch was anything but whole-hearted. The opening months of Richard's reign, as he disposed of his critics and enemies, saw five executions, and this made London an uneasy place to be. 'There is much trouble,' reported one newsletter to the provinces, 'and every man doubts the other.'

The new king's favourites ruled the roost, and Richard's roster of unpopular sidekicks prompted a famous piece of doggerel:

> *The Cat, the Rat, and Lovell our Dog*
> *Rule all England under the Hog.*

The Cat was Sir William Catesby, a sharp-witted lawyer who was Speaker of the House of Commons — his job it was to make sure that MPs toed the line with the new regime. The Rat was Sir Richard Ratcliffe, one of Richard's oldest cronies; Francis, Lord Lovell, who had a silver dog on his crest, had grown up with Richard in the household of Warwick the Kingmaker; and the Hog was Richard himself — a derisive reference to the white boar of his crest.

Today it is our sacred right to make fun of our rulers. Satirists and cheeky impersonators make up a major branch of the entertainment business, sometimes becoming so famous in their own right that they outshine the national leaders they deride. But things were very different in 1484, when the authorities tracked down Sir William Collingbourne, the Wiltshire gentleman who had dared pen the scornful verse that had ended up pinned to the door of St Paul's Cathedral. Collingbourne was one of several West-Countrymen accused of plotting rebellion, and while the others were spared, the lampooner received special treatment for his 'rhyme [in] derision of the king and his council'.

He was strung up on the gallows, then cut down while still breathing, to be castrated and disembowelled.

To his credit, Collingbourne seems to have retained his sense of humour to the end. 'Oh Lord Jesus, yet more trouble,' he sighed, as the executioner reached inside his body to yank out his intestines.

THE BATTLE OF
BOSWORTH FIELD

1485

ONE DAY IN THE SUMMER OF 1485, THE
French chronicler Philippe de Commynes encoun-
tered Henry Tudor at the court of the King of France. It was
the young Welshman's latest port of call in more than
twenty years of exile. Moving from castle to castle across
Brittany and France, he knew what it was to live from hand
to mouth. From the time he was five years old, Henry told
the Frenchman, he 'had always been a fugitive or a prisoner'.

Now all this was about to change. With his faithful uncle
Jasper Tudor beside him, Henry was preparing his bid for
the English throne. Since Richard III had seized power two
years earlier, an increasing trickle of Englishmen had been

making their way across the Channel to throw in their lot with the young man whose descent through his mother Lady Margaret Beaufort — and, to a lesser extent, through his grandfather Owen's romantic marriage to Queen Catherine of France — made Henry the best alternative to Richard.

On 1 August Henry set sail with a force of a thousand or so soldiers, including a group of French pikemen he was paying with borrowed funds. They were heading for the south-west tip of Wales, Jasper's home territory, where Henry himself had been born, and they dropped anchor in Milford Haven on Sunday the 7th. Their plan was to head north in a loop across Wales, gathering support as they marched. Local poets, we are told, had been primed to proclaim the coming of *y mab darogan*, 'the man of destiny'.

In the event, the response was far from overwhelming. Few Welshmen were willing to risk their lives on Henry's threadbare enterprise, and when he reached Shrewsbury and the English Midlands there was further disappointment. Henry had been counting on the support of his stepfather, his mother's third husband Thomas, Lord Stanley. But anticipating such a move, Richard III had seized Stanley's eldest son and was holding him hostage.

The Stanley family certainly had the power to determine the course of the forthcoming conflict — they were the major magnates in the area. But they had not achieved their standing by taking chances. In battle, they had a history of holding back their troops till the very last possible moment — and in the high summer of 1485 this was as far as they were prepared to go for young Henry. When the armies of Henry Tudor and Richard III finally confronted each other on

Monday 22 August, Henry's forces were considerably out-numbered by those of the King — though Richard's army also lacked the reinforcements he had been promised, with the Stanleys keeping their troops on the side.

Tradition has set the momentous Battle of Bosworth Field not far from Leicester. But modern research suggests that the armies may have clashed several miles further west near the modern A5 and the village of Mancetter, just north of Coventry, where Boadicea made her last stand fourteen hundred years earlier. The A5 follows the great curve of Watling Street, the Roman road connecting London with north Wales. So as Henry's pikemen made their uncertain way towards Richard's army, they were tracing the route of the Roman legions.

By one account, Richard was plagued by bad dreams and premonitions on the night before the battle. But he put on a brave face. He clad himself ostentatiously in glorious kingly armour, setting the gold circlet of the crown over his helmet. Then, when he caught sight of his rival's standard at the back of the Tudor army, he launched a cavalry charge directly at it.

'This day I will die as a king,' he cried, 'or win.'

There is some speculation as to why Henry was stationed to the rear of his men. The cautious claimant seems to have had an eye to cutting his losses if the battle went against him — he had left his uncle, Jasper, even further to the rear to cover his getaway. But Henry was saved by his French pikemen, who presented Richard's charging horsemen with a tactic never before seen in England. Swiftly, they formed their five-metre-plus steel-headed staves into a bristling defensive wall around their leader, and as Richard's cavalry hit the pike wall, the King was unhorsed. An eyewitness account by one of the mercenaries, written the day after the battle and recently rediscovered in a nineteenth-century transcription, describes Richard crying out in rage and frustration: 'These French traitors are today the cause of our realm's ruin!'

This seems to have been the moment that prompted the Stanleys, at last, to intervene. Cagey as ever, Lord Stanley himself continued to hold back, but his brother Sir William deftly moved his troops across the battlefield, overpowering Richard's soldiers and cornering the King. Richard fought on, bravely refusing his friends' offer of a horse on which to flee.

'A horse! A horse! My kingdom for a horse!' Shakespeare's *Tragedy of King Richard III* dramatically portrays the hunchback monarch screaming for a fresh mount to carry him to the personal showdown he craved with Henry Tudor. And in this depiction of defiant courage, the playwright finally does right by the King. By most eyewitness and contemporary accounts, Richard fought to the very last, until he was finally overpowered and cut down, his crown rolling off his helmet as he fell. Sir William Stanley picked up the gold circlet and placed it on Henry Tudor's head. 'Sir, here I make you King of England.'

As always after a battle, the victors turned to plunder. Stanley was allowed to take whatever he wished from the dead king's tent — he picked out a set of royal tapestries for the Stanley residence, enduring evidence of the family's decisive, if less than heroic, doings on Bosworth Field.

Richard's miniature Book of Hours, his beautifully illustrated personal prayer book, went to Henry's mother Lady Margaret — while Henry himself chose to keep the delicate gold crown.

Richard's corpse, meanwhile, was stripped of all clothing — 'naught being left about him so much as would cover his privy member'. The body was then slung over a horse, with arms and legs hanging down on both sides, 'trussed . . . as a hog or other vile beast and so all bespattered with mire and filth'. He was taken to the Greyfriars Church at Leicester, and there he was buried 'without any pomp or solemn funeral'.

Five decades later the tomb was broken open when the friary was destroyed during the Dissolution of the Monasteries. To this day, the bones that are said to have belonged to the little Princes in the Tower rest in honour in Westminster Abbey. But sometime in the 1530s the bones of Richard III were thrown into a river in Leicestershire.

DOUBLE TROUBLE

1486-99

ON 18 JANUARY 1486 THE NEW KING HENRY VII, the twenty-eight-year-old victor of Bosworth, married nineteen-year-old Princess Elizabeth of York, the elder sister of the tragic Princes in the Tower. Plotted by Henry's mother, Margaret Beaufort, the marriage was a step towards mending the bitter and bloodstained rift between the House of Lancaster and the House of York.

But the mysterious disappearance of the little princes had left a curious legacy. No one could be quite sure what had happened to them — and, if they *had* been murdered, who was to blame. Despite the suspicion attaching to Richard

III, there were no bodies and no closure: the poison had not been drawn. For a dozen years England was haunted by conspiracy theories made flesh. It was the age of the pretenders.

The first was Lambert Simnel, an Oxford tradesman's son who became the tool of Richard Symonds, an ambitious local priest. Symonds took his twelve-year-old protégé to Ireland, claiming that Simnel was Edward, Earl of Warwick, the young nephew of Richard III (see Wars of the Roses family tree, p. x). On Whit Sunday 1487 'King Edward VI' was crowned by dissident Irish noblemen in Dublin.

The real Edward was in the Tower of London. Henry had made it a priority to put Warwick away when he came to the throne, and now he lost no time in bringing him out to be paraded through the streets of London. When Simnel and his Irish followers landed at Furness in Lancashire later that June, Henry marched north to defeat them in a rerun of the previous years of disorder.

But the Tudor response in victory was a new departure. Instead of executing 'Edward VI', Henry gave Simnel a job in the royal kitchens, turning the spit that roasted the royal ox. The boy made such a good job of his duties as a scullion that he rapidly earned promotion, rising to take care of Henry's beloved hunting hawks and finishing up as royal falconer.

In his humane, rather humorous treatment of Lambert Simnel, Henry was making a point — this new king did not kill children. He even spared the boy's Svengali, Symonds, who had planned to have himself made Archbishop of Canterbury. But Henry might have done better to be more severe, for within a few years he was confronted with another pretender. This one declared himself to be Richard, Duke of York, the younger of the Princes in the Tower. Apparently, he had made a miraculous escape following his elder brother's murder and had now returned to claim the throne.

'King Richard IV' — by this account, Henry's brother-in-law — would later confess that he was, in fact, one Pierquin Wesbecque (Perkin Warbeck) from Tournai in the Netherlands, the son of a boatman. But it suited all manner of people to believe he was indeed the nephew of Richard III, and he did the rounds of Henry's enemies and neighbours, being treated to banquets and hunting excursions and given money to buy troops. King James IV of Scotland even found him an attractive wife, his own cousin Lady Katherine Gordon.

This pretender's six-year odyssey came to grief in the autumn of 1497, after a failed attempt to raise the West Country against Henry. Captured at Beaulieu in Hampshire, he finally admitted his humble origins. But having heard his confession, Henry again took a conciliatory line, inviting Warbeck and his charming Scottish wife to join his court. It was as if the King was enjoying the fairytale himself. Even when Warbeck tried to escape the following summer, Henry was content merely to put him in the stocks and have him repeat his confession. It was not until Warbeck tried to escape yet again that the King lost patience. On 23 November 1499 the false claimant was hanged, and a few days later the true claimant, the hapless Earl of Warwick, was beheaded on Tower Hill.

Henry gave Warbeck's noble widow a pension and made her lady-in-waiting to the Queen. Lady Katherine Gordon became quite a figure at the Tudor court, marrying no fewer than three more husbands and surviving until 1537. But the King's sharp dose of reality in 1499 had the desired effect — no more pretenders.

FISH 'N' SHIPS

1497

In fourteen hundred ninety-two, Columbus sailed the ocean blue
And found this land, land of the Free, beloved by you, beloved by me.

FOURTEEN NINETY-TWO IS THE FAMOUS DATE when Christopher Columbus is credited by history with the 'discovery' of America. But modern archaeologists have shown that the Vikings must have crossed the Atlantic long before him. The remains of Viking homes, cooking pits and metal ornaments on the island of Newfoundland have been dated to around the year 1000. And there is every reason to believe that Columbus was also preceded to the Americas by several shiploads of weather-beaten Englishmen.

The men had set sail from Bristol, heading out from the prosperous port on the River Avon in the west of England, first towards Ireland, then further westwards into the Atlantic. They were fishermen, searching for cod that they could salt and trade for wine, and they brought back tales of remote islands that they called 'The Isle of the Seven Cities' and 'The Isle of Brasil'. Late in the 1490s an English merchant called John Day reported their discoveries to the 'Grand Admiral' of Spain — the *Almirante Major* — who may have been Columbus himself. In a letter that was misfiled for centuries in the National Archives at Simancas, Day pointed out that the New World across the Atlantic had, in fact, already been 'found and discovered in other times by the men of Bristol . . . as your Lordship knows'.

The problem with this English claim to transatlantic discovery is that these West Country fishermen had kept their find to themselves, as cagey fishermen tend to do. Harbour records make clear that in the 1480s, if not earlier, ships from Bristol had located the fabulously fecund Grand Banks fishing grounds that lie off New England and Newfoundland. But they did not wish to attract competitors or poachers. Their only interest in terra firma of any sort was as a landmark to guide them to the fishing waters. So Christopher Columbus has retained the glory for 1492 — and in any case, 'discovery' now seems the wrong word for landing on a continent that was already occupied by hundreds of thousands, if not millions, of indigenous American Indians.

When a contingent of Bristolians did finally set foot in America in a properly documented fashion, they did so under royal patronage. Around 1494 an Italian navigator, Zuan Caboto, arrived at the court of King Henry VII. Like Columbus, Caboto came from Genoa and he was a skilled propagandist for the exploding world of discovery. Brandishing charts and an impressive globe, he persuaded Henry to grant him a charter to 'seeke out, discover and finde whatsoever isles, countries, regions or provinces of heathens and infidels . . . which before this time have been unknown to all Christians'.

The prudent king was not about to invest any of his own money in the project. On the contrary, royal approval carried a price tag — 20 per cent of the profits. But Zuan, now 'John Cabot', was granted permanent tax exemption on whatever he might bring back from the New World for himself. So he went down to Bristol in search of investors. There he was able to fit out a small wooden sailing ship, the *Matthew*, with a crew of eighteen, most of them 'hearty Bristol sailors'.

It might seem surprising that the clannish West-Countrymen should team up with an Italian, an outsider, but there was a fraternity among those who risked their lives on the mysterious western ocean. Cabot was skilled in the latest navigational techniques using the stars, and he needed a crew who would not lose their nerve when out of sight of land for four weeks or more.

In the event, the journey took five. On 24 June 1497, thirty-five days after leaving England, the *Matthew* sighted land and dropped anchor somewhere off the coast of modern Newfoundland, Labrador or Nova Scotia. Cautiously,

Cabot and his landing party rowed ashore, where they found the remains of a fire, some snares set for game, a needle for making nets and a trail that headed inland. Obviously, there were humans around; but Cabot was not keen to meet them. 'Since he was with just a few people,' John Day later explained in his letter to the Spanish Grand Admiral, 'he did not dare advance inland beyond the shooting distance of a crossbow.'

The landing party planted four banners: the arms of St George, on behalf of King Henry VII; a papal banner on behalf of the Pope; the flag of Venice, since Cabot had taken Venetian citizenship; and a cross intended for the local 'heathens and infidels'. Then the English mariners set off down the coast in pursuit of their great passion — the waters were 'swarming with fish', Cabot later boasted to the Milanese Ambassador, and there was no need of a net to catch them: they could just lean over the ship's rail and 'let down baskets with a stone'.

Heading for home around the middle of July, captain and crew used the same method that had got them there — the so-called 'dead reckoning'. This involved fixing on one particular angle to the stars and preserving that angle as they sailed, effectively staying on one line of latitude as they moved around the curve of the globe. Contrary to received wisdom, fifteenth-century sailors did not believe the world was flat. Indeed, its roundness was the basis of their adventurous navigation techniques.

By 23 August, Cabot was back in London, reporting on his finds to the King who, never careless with his money, doled out an immediate ten pounds — about four times the average annual wage at the time. Henry also granted the mariner an annual pension of twenty pounds for life, to be paid by the port of Bristol out of its customs receipts. But John Cabot did not live to claim it. The next year he set out on another expedition westwards where, as the Tudor historian Polydore Vergil heartlessly put it, the 'newe founde lande' he discovered was 'nowhere but on the very bottom of the ocean'. Cabot and his ship vanished without trace.

But his death did not discourage other adventurers. In 1501 Henry VII commissioned six more Bristolians to head westwards, and they returned with Arctic hunting falcons — perhaps the King gave them to Lambert Simnel to train — along with a few of the native inhabitants that Cabot had been careful to avoid encountering four years earlier: 'They were clothed in beasts' skins and ate raw flesh,' recorded one awestruck chronicler, 'and spake such speech that no man could understand them . . . In their demeanour [they were] like . . . brute beasts.'

Falcons, fish and Eskimos — as the Inuit people came to be called at the end of the sixteenth century — were interesting enough, but they bore no comparison to the gold, jewels and, above all, silver that Spain would soon be carrying home in heaving galleon-loads from the southerly lands discovered by Columbus. It would be more than seventy years before England made a determined effort to settle the northern parts of the continent that, after 1507, would be described on the maps as 'America'.

But the Eskimos settled in nicely, thank you. They evidently found themselves a tailor, for just two years after they had first appeared at Henry's court in their animal skins, England's first New World immigrants were spotted by a chronicler strolling around the Palace of Westminster, 'apparelled after the manner of Englishmen'. They were no longer 'brute beasts', he admitted — 'I could not discern [them] from Englishmen.'

FORK IN, FORK OUT

1500

FOR MORE THAN HALF HIS REIGN, HENRY VII's chief minister was Cardinal John Morton, Archbishop of Canterbury and one of the great church statesmen who shaped England's story during the Middle Ages. Often of lowly birth, these clever individuals rose through the meritocratic system of ecclesiastical education to make their names — in Morton's case, via the challenging task of national fund-raising.

When collecting money for the King, Morton's commissioners are said to have confronted their targets with a truly undodgeable means test. If a likely customer appeared prosperous, he obviously had surplus funds to contribute to the

King's coffers. If, on the other hand, he lived modestly, he must have been stashing his wealth away. Either way the victim was compelled to pay — impaled, as it were, upon one or other of the twin prongs of a pitchfork.

Like many of history's chestnuts, the facts behind what came to be known as 'Morton's Fork' are not quite as neat as the story. It was more than 130 years later that the statesman-philosopher Francis Bacon coined the phrase, and the documents of the time make clear that Morton did not wield the pitchfork personally. But the cardinal certainly did work hard to satisfy the appetite of a money-hungry monarch. As well as helping Henry to tighten up parliamentary taxation, he presided over the collection of 'benevolences' — 'voluntary' wealth taxes that invited subjects to show their goodwill towards the King. Not surprisingly, these forced loans soon became known as 'malevolences', and Henry himself developed a reputation as a miser. 'In his later days,' wrote the normally loyal Polydore Vergil, 'all [his] virtues were obscured by avarice.'

Henry VII's account ledgers would seem to bear this out. At the foot of page after page are the royal initials, scratched by the careful bookkeeper monarch as he ran his finger down the columns. But Henry could spend lavishly when he wanted to, particularly when it came to making his kingship visibly magnificent. In November 1501 he spent £14,000 (over £8 million today) on jewels alone for the wedding in St Paul's Cathedral of his eldest son Arthur to Katherine of Aragon, daughter of Ferdinand and Isabella of Spain. Ten days of tournaments were staged at Westminster and the feasting went on night after night beneath the hammer-beam roof of the Great Hall, the walls hung with the costliest cloth of Arras.

Two years later Henry splashed out again when he sent his daughter Margaret north to marry King James IV of Scotland, with an escort of two thousand horsemen, a train of magnificently clad noblemen and £16,000 (another £9 million or so) in jewels. Henry VII's marriage-broking proved portentous. It was Margaret's marriage that would one day bring the Stuart dynasty to England, while Katherine of Aragon, following the death of Arthur in 1502, would be passed on as wife to his younger brother Henry, with equally historic consequences.

Henry VII had done well by England when he died, aged fifty-two, in April 1509. You can see his death mask in Westminster Abbey, his face lean and intelligent, his eyes sharp and his mouth shut, concealing the teeth which, according to contemporary description, were 'few, poor and black-stained'. He lies in splendour in the magnificent chapel that he built at the south end of the abbey — another notable item of dynastic extravagance. Beside him lies his wife Elizabeth of York, and not far away, his mother Lady Margaret Beaufort, who had schemed so hard and faithfully to bring her Tudor son to power.

The soaring stone pillars of the chapel are decorated with the Beaufort portcullis and with the double rose that would become the symbol of the Tudors, giving graphic shape to the healing, but oversimplified, myth that the warring flowers had been melded into a flourishing new hybrid. One of the chapel's stained-glass windows shows a crown wreathed in a thorn bush, and later legend relates how Henry actually plucked his crown from such a bush at Bosworth. In fact, contemporary accounts of the battle made no mention of bushes — they describe the crown as simply being picked up off the ground. But it is fair enough to think of Henry as the King who redeemed England from a thorny situation.

KING HENRY VIII'S
'GREAT MATTER'

1509‑33

AFTER THE PENNY-PINCHING WAYS OF
Henry VII, the profligate glamour of his red-blooded,
redheaded son, the new King Henry VIII, exploded over
England like a sunburst. Just seventeen years old, the athletic young monarch was the nation's sporting hero.

'It is the prettiest thing in the world to see him play,'
purred an admirer of Henry's exertions at tennis, 'his fair
skin glowing through a shirt of the finest texture.' When the
young King, tall and energetic, joined the royal bowmen for
target practice, his arrow 'cleft the mark in the middle and
surpassed them all'. He was a superlative horseman, a champion in the jousts, an all-round wrestler — and when the

music started, he could pluck a mean string on the lute. Recent research has revealed that Henry may even have played football, a game usually considered too rough and common for the well born. In February 2004 a fresh look at the inventory of his Great Wardrobe discovered that alongside forty-five pairs of velvet shoes the King kept a pair of purpose-made football boots.

The other side of bluff King Hal was evident within three days of his accession. With the vicious eye for a scapegoat that was to characterise his ruling style, the King authorised the show trials of Richard Empson and Edmund Dudley, two of his father's most effective and unpopular money-raisers. The pair had done nothing worse than carry out royal orders and line their own pockets. But Henry had both men executed — then promptly embarked on a spending spree with his father's carefully hoarded treasure. He had an insatiable capacity for enjoying himself. Masques, mummeries, jousts, pageants — the festivities went on for days when Henry was crowned in June 1509 alongside his fetching and prestigious new Spanish wife Katherine of Aragon.

Four years older than Henry, Katherine was embarking on her second marriage. Having married Henry's brother Arthur in November 1501, she had found herself widowed before that winter was out. Young Henry had stepped forward to take Arthur's place both as Prince of Wales and as Katherine's betrothed, and when he came to the throne he made their marriage his first order of personal business. The couple exchanged vows and rings in a private ceremony at Greenwich on 11 June 1509, and set about the happy process of procreation. When, after one miscarriage, a son was born on New Year's Day 1511, Henry's joy knew no bounds. As bonfires were lit and salutes cannonaded from the Tower, the proud father staged a vast tournament, mingling with the crowds and delightedly allowing them to tear off as souvenirs the splendid gold letters 'H' and 'K' that adorned his clothes.

But the baby boy, who had been christened Henry, died within two months, and disappointment would prove the pattern of Katherine's childbearing. One daughter, Mary, born in 1516, was the only healthy survivor of a succession of ill-fated pregnancies, births and stillbirths, and after ten years of marriage without a male heir, Henry came to ponder on the reasons for God's displeasure.

He thought he found his answer in the Bible. 'Thou shalt not uncover the nakedness of thy brother's wife,' read chapter 18 of the Old Testament Book of Leviticus — and two chapters later, the consequences were set out clearly: 'If a man shall take his brother's wife, it is an unclean thing . . . they shall be childless.' This apparently firm prohibition had been overruled at the time of Henry and Katherine's betrothal in 1504 by special licence from the Pope, who based his action on the contradictory instruction in the Book of Deuteronomy that it was a man's duty to take his brother's widow 'and raise up seed for his brother'. Katherine, for her part, firmly maintained that she was free to marry Henry because her five-month marriage to the fifteen-year-old Arthur had never been consummated.

But as Katherine remained childless through the 1520s, her discontented husband started to lend a ready ear to those who suggested that his wife could easily have been lying. 'Bring me a cup of ale,' brother Arthur was said to have cried out contentedly on the first morning of his married life, 'I have been this night in the midst of Spain!'

To Henry the solution seemed simple. Since a pope had fixed his improper, heirless marriage to Katherine, a pope should now unfix it, freeing the English King to take the fertile young wife his dynastic duty required — and by the spring of 1527 the thirty-six-year-old Henry knew exactly who that wife should be. He had fallen in love with Anne Boleyn, a self-assured beauty ten years or so his junior, notable for a pair of mesmeric dark eyes and a steely sense of purpose.

But as Henry set his mind to making a new marriage, events in Italy made it highly unlikely that the Pope would give him any help. In May that year Rome was captured and sacked by the troops of Charles V, the powerful Habsburg ruler who was also Katherine's nephew. Charles controlled Spain, the Netherlands, much of Germany and Italy — and now the Pope. There was no way he would allow his aunt to be humiliatingly cast aside by the King of England.

Until now Henry had been content to leave the handling of his divorce to Cardinal Thomas Wolsey, the talented church statesman who ran the country for him, as Cardinal Morton had taken care of business for his father. But the normally competent cardinal was left helpless after the shift of power in Rome — and he had made the mistake of offending the now powerful Anne Boleyn. He called her the 'night crow'. After fourteen years of effectively running England, Wolsey was disgraced. Charged with treason, he died from the shock. Henry took over Hampton Court, the magnificent palace the portly cardinal had built for himself down the Thames from Richmond — and started lending an ear to advisers who were considerably more Popo-sceptic.

Chief among these was Anne herself, who had a radical taste in reading. Sometime in 1530 she placed in Henry's hands a copy of the recently published *Obedience of a Christian Man* by the reformer William Tyndale, a controversial little volume that had been denounced as 'a holy boke of disobedyence' by Thomas More, Wolsey's successor as Lord Chancellor. *How Christian Rulers Ought to Govern* was Tyndale's subtitle, and he argued that, since the Bible made no mention of the Pope (nor of bishops, abbots, church courts or of the whole earthly edifice of church power and glory), the Church should be governed like the state, by a 'true Christian prince' — without interference from the so-called 'Bishop of Rome'.

'This book is for me and for all Kings to read,' mused Henry — here was the solution to his troublesome 'Great Matter'. Why should the King not effectively award himself his own divorce, as governor of the English Church, in order to secure the heir that his country needed? 'England cares nothing for popes,' Anne's brother George Boleyn would declare to a papal official visiting England in the summer of 1530. 'The king is absolute emperor and pope in his own kingdom.'

The Boleyns were thrusting members of the rising Tudor gentry — landowners and former merchants whose personal beliefs were traditional but who had no special fondness for the Pope, and still less for the power and privileges of the clergy with their unearned wealth and their special exemptions from the law. Scrounging was the Church's speciality, according to a scurrilous tract of the time, *A Supplication for the Beggars*, which pretended to be a petition from the 'Beggars of England' to the King, complaining that crafty churchmen were putting them out of business by begging so much better than they could. Stealing land, money and even, on occasion, the virtue of good men's wives and daughters, the clerics had filched 'the whole realm', complained the *Supplication*.

This jeering anticlerical sentiment was mobilised in the autumn of 1529, when Parliament gathered for what was to prove an historic series of sessions. Discontented laymen were invited to draw up lists of their grievances against the clergy, and the result, finally codified in May 1532, was a formidable roundup of just about everything that people found irritating about the often complacent and greedy ways of the all-too-earthly Church. It was exactly what the King wanted to hear. 'We thought that the clergy of our realm had been our subjects wholly,' declared Henry menacingly as he studied the list of complaints. 'But now we have well perceived that they be but half our subjects.'

Here was an area where the King and a fair number of the merchants, lawyers, country gentlemen and landed magnates who dominated Parliament clearly felt as one. England, they argued, should have control over its own Church — and between 1529 and 1536 Parliament passed a series of laws to accomplish that, transferring the many aspects of church life and business to the Crown.

The immediate consequence was that Henry was able to marry Anne and cast off Katherine. But the long-term consequence of these new laws went far beyond Henry and his need for a son. 'This realm of England is an empire . . .' declared the Act in Restraint of Appeals of 1533, 'governed by one supreme head and king . . . furnished with plenary, whole and entire power . . . without restraint or provocation to any foreign princes or potentates of the world'.

Henry's 'Great Matter' turned out to be greater than anyone, including himself, had guessed. English kings now acknowledged no superior under God on earth.

'LET THERE BE LIGHT' —
WILLIAM TYNDALE AND
THE ENGLISH BIBLE

1525

HENRY VIII'S HISTORIC BREAK WITH ROME was fundamentally about earthly power, not spiritual belief. Even while Henry was demolishing the Pope's authority over the English Church in the early 1530s, a Sunday service in the average English parish was still shaped by the comforting chants and Catholic rituals hallowed by the centuries.

But in Europe, belief was changing more radically. In October 1517 the rebellious German monk Martin Luther, a miner's son turned theologian and philosophy professor, had nailed his famous ninety-five theses — or 'propositions' — to the church door in Wittenberg in Saxony. Luther was appalled by the materialism of the Roman Church, and his ninety-five propositions were a particular attack on the sale of 'indulgences', Church-approved coupons that people purchased in the belief that they were being let off their sins — printed tickets to heaven. The Pope had no authority to forgive people's sins, argued Luther, let alone offer forgiveness for sale, like bread or beer. It was faith alone that would bring salvation, and men had no need of priests to mediate with God. Believers could commune directly with their Maker through prayer, and by reading God's word in the Bible. Within a few years several dozen of Germany's duchies and principalities had thrown off papal authority and signed up to Luther's protests and to his call for reform — generating the movement that historians would later call the Protestant Reformation.

Henry VIII was outraged. He thought that Luther's views undermined civil obedience, and left people with no reason to be good. When Luther's message reached England, the King was still on warm terms with the Pope, and with the help of Thomas More he fired off an indignant diatribe against the heretical German, earning himself the title *Fidei Defensor*, 'Defender of the Faith'. To this day the abbreviations *Fid. Def.*, or *F.D.*, appear on the face of every English coin, commemorating the title by which in 1521, only a decade before the break with Rome, the grateful Pope declared Henry his favourite and most faithful prince in Europe. On Henry's orders, Cardinal Wolsey organised public burnings of Luther's books, and even hunted down the reformer's translation of the New Testament into German.

The Roman Church's own version of the Bible was in Latin — the fourth-century Latin of St Jerome, whose precise meaning might be accessible to learned priests and scholars but which floated sonorously over the heads of most churchgoers, rather like a magical incantation, heavy on comfort and light on explanation. The Roman priesthood's control over faith relied heavily on its virtual monopoly of Latin, and most churchmen felt deeply threatened by the idea of people reading the Bible in their own language and interpreting it for themselves.

But this was precisely the ambition of the young priest, William Tyndale, who was working in Gloucestershire in the early 1520s. This area, on the border with Wales, had long been a stronghold of the Lollards, the prayer-mumbling disciples of John Wycliffe who, back in the 1380s, had argued that the Bible should be made accessible to ordinary people in their own tongue. 'If God spare my life,' declared Tyndale in a heated argument with an establishment cleric who had railed against the translating of the Bible, 'ere many years, I wyl cause a boye that dryveth the plough, shall know more the Scripture than thou dost.'

The talented and scholarly Tyndale had command of eight languages, notably Greek and Hebrew, which were virtually unknown in England at this time. He was also blessed with an extraordinary ability to create poetic phrases in his native tongue, and his memorable translations live on to this day — 'the salt of the earth', 'signs of the times', 'the powers that be' and even 'bald as a coot' we owe to William Tyndale. All these vibrant expressions flowed from his pen as, through the 1520s, he laboured to render the word of God into ploughboy language. When he could not find the right word, he invented it — 'scapegoat' and 'broken-hearted' are two of his coinages. As he translated, he was helping to shape the very rhythm and thought patterns of English: 'eat drink and be merry' — 'am I my brother's keeper?' — 'fight the good fight' — 'blessed are the meek for they shall inherit the earth' . . .

To avoid the wrath of Wolsey, who was having heretics whipped and imprisoned, Tyndale had to compose his fine phrases abroad. In 1524 he travelled to Europe, where he dodged from printing press to printing press in cities like Hamburg and Brussels — shadowed by the cardinal's agents, who had identified this prolific wordsmith as a home-grown heretic quite as dangerous as Luther. In 1526, Tyndale managed to get three thousand copies of his New Testament printed in the German city of Worms, and within months the books were circulating among freethinkers in England, smuggled in by Hull sailors in casks of wax and grain. It was four years later that a copy of Tyndale's *Obedience of a Christian Man* reached Anne Boleyn, providing encouragement for Henry's break from the Pope.

But then in 1530, Tyndale dared to address the great question of the King's marriage from a biblical point of view, and with the perversity of the dyed-in-the-wool nonconformist he concluded in his book *The Practice of Prelates* that the Bible did *not* authorise Henry to jettison his wife.

It was his death sentence. The growing number of reformers among the English clergy were advocating the use of the Bible in English, and Tyndale's accurate and powerful translation was the obvious version to use. But the King was infuriated by Tyndale's criticism of his divorce and of his proposed marriage to Anne. The English agents kept up their pursuit of the fugitive, and in May 1535 they got their man. Now aged about forty, he was captured in Antwerp, to be condemned as a heretic and sentenced to be burned to death.

On 6 October 1536, William Tyndale was led out to his execution. As a small token of mercy he was granted the kindness of being strangled in the moments before the fire was lit. But the executioner bungled the tightening of the rope, painfully crushing Tyndale's throat while leaving him still alive as the flames licked around him.

'Lord, open the King of England's eyes!' cried the reformer as he died.

The executioner piled on more fuel until the body was totally consumed, since the purpose of burning heretics was to reduce them to ashes that could be thrown to the winds — no trace of their presence should be left on earth. But William Tyndale left more than ashes: 'In the begynnynge was the worde and the worde was with God and the worde was God . . . In it was lyfe and the lyfe was the light of men. And the light shyneth in the darknes, but the darknes comprehended it not.'

THOMAS MORE AND HIS
WONDERFUL 'NO-PLACE'

1535

YOUNG HENRY VIII LOVED THE COMPANY OF
the learned and witty Thomas More. The King would
take him up on to the roof of his palace to gaze skywards
and 'consider with him the diversities, courses, motions and
operations of the stars'. Travelling in his barge down the
Thames one day, he decided to drop in unexpectedly on the
Mores' sprawling riverside home in Chelsea. He invited
himself for dinner, then walked in the garden with his host
'by the space of an hour, holding his arm about his neck'.

More's son-in-law William Roper was much impressed
by this intimacy with the King, but More himself had no il-
lusions. 'Son Roper, I may tell thee...' he confided, 'if my

head could win His Majesty a castle in France it should not fail to go.'

Thomas More was literally a Renaissance man, playing his own part in the great 're-birthing' of the fifteenth and sixteenth centuries. South of the Alps, the Renaissance was famously embodied by such artists as Michelangelo and Leonardo. In the north, it was the so-called 'Christian humanists' like More and his Dutch friend Erasmus who struck sparks off each other — to memorable effect. In 1509, Erasmus dedicated his great work *In Praise of Folly* to Thomas (its Latin name, *Encomium Moriae*, was a pun on More's name). More responded with his own flight of intellect, *Utopia* — his inspired combination of the Greek words for 'no' and 'place'.

Utopia is the tale More claimed to have heard when, coming out of church one day, he bumped into an old seaman: 'his face was tanned, he had a long beard, and his cloak was hanging carelessly about him'. This philosopher-sailor had been travelling with the Italian explorer Amerigo Vespucci, after whom the Americas would shortly be named. Having chatted with More for a while about all that was presently wrong with the kingdoms of Europe, he started describing his experiences on the island of 'Utopia' where, he said, there was no shortage of life's essentials. When people went to the market, everything was free, and because of that 'there is no danger of a man's asking for more than he needs . . . since they are sure that they shall always be supplied. It is the fear of want that makes any of the whole race of animals either greedy or ravenous.'

Like space travel in our own day, the sixteenth century's voyages of discovery were stirring people's imaginations, and

More's *Utopia* was a sort of science fiction, a fantasy about a super-perfect society where thoughtful people had worked out a life of benevolent equality. In this ideal 'No-Place', couples who were 'more fruitful' shared their children with those who were not so blessed, while lawyers were totally banned — they were a profession who disguised the truth, explained More quizzically, whose own wealth came from his prosperous legal practice. Living according to nature, striving for health and dying cheerfully, the Utopians offered a satirical commentary on the 'moth-eaten' laws and the hypocrisy of European society — and More himself tried to put some of Utopia's ideas into practice, encouraging his daughters to debate philosophy in front of him. 'Erudition in women is a new thing,' he wrote, 'and a reproach to the idleness of men.'

But More's visionary thinking was tethered to a deep religious conservatism — he was steadfastly loyal to the Pope and to the old ways of the Church. In the style of Thomas Becket, he wore a hair shirt beneath the glorious liveries of the public offices that he occupied — though unlike Becket, he kept his prickly garment maggot-free: it was regularly laundered by his daughter Margaret Roper. Thomas shared his royal master Henry VIII's indignation at Martin Luther and his reforming ideas, outdoing the King in his furious invective. In one diatribe, More described Luther as *merda, stercus, lutum, coenum* — shit, dung, filth, excrement. And for good measure, he then denounced the German as a drunkard, a liar, an ape and an arsehole who had been vomited on to this earth by the Antichrist.

More joined Henry's Council in 1517, the same year that Luther nailed his theses to the church door in Wittenberg,

and set about waging a personal war on the new ideas for reform. He had a little jail and a set of stocks built in his garden so he could cross-question heretics personally, and he
nursed a particular hatred for the translations of William
Tyndale, whom he described as 'a hell-hound in the kennel
of the devil'. When More got back to Chelsea after his work
on the King's Council he would spend his evenings penning
harangues denouncing Tyndale, while defending the traditional practices of the Church.

But while More and Tyndale might differ over popes and
sacraments, they were agreed on the subject of kings' wives.
More actually shared Tyndale's opinion that the Bible did
not authorise Henry VIII's annulment of his marriage with
Katherine — and their highly inconvenient conviction set
both men on a tragic collision course with the King. When,
after the disgrace of Wolsey, Henry invited Thomas to become his new Lord Chancellor, More at first refused. He
could see the danger ahead. He only accepted after Henry
promised not to embroil him in the divorce, leaving the 'Great
Matter' to those 'whose consciences could well enough agree
therein'.

But detachment became impossible as Henry's quarrel
with the Pope grew more bitter. By the early 1530s royal policy was being guided by the gimlet-eyed Thomas Cromwell,
a former agent of Wolsey's who, in the spring of 1534, pushed
a new statute through Parliament, the Act of Succession.
This required men to swear their agreement to the settlement, rejecting the rights of Katherine and her daughter
Mary. When More refused to swear, he was promptly escorted to the Tower.

'By the mass, Master More,' warned the Duke of Norfolk, an old friend and one of several visitors who tried to persuade him to change his mind, 'it is perilous striving with princes . . . I would wish you somewhat to incline to the king's pleasure for, by God's body, *indignatio principis mors est* — the wrath of the king is death.'

'Is that all, my lord?' responded Thomas. 'Then in good faith is there no more difference between your Grace and me, but that I shall die today and you tomorrow.'

More was led out to the scaffold early on the morning of 6 July 1535, and he kept up his graceful, ironic humour to the end. 'I pray you, Master Lieutenant, see me safe up,' he said as he mounted the ladder, 'and [for] my coming down, let me shift for myself.'

Worn and thin from his months in prison, loose in his clothes, with a skullcap on his head and a long straggling beard, the former chancellor looked not unlike the old sailor-philosopher he had once imagined telling stories of 'No-Place' — and that name he invented for his imaginary island remains to this day the word people use when they want to describe a wonderful but impossible dream.

DIVORCED, BEHEADED, DIED . . .

1533–7

ANNE BOLEYN SAILED DOWN THE THAMES to her coronation at the end of May 1533 in a Cleopatra's fleet of vessels. Anne herself rode in Katherine of Aragon's former barge — from which the discarded Queen's coat of arms had been hacked away — and her costume made clear the reason for her triumph. The new Queen had added 'a panel to her skirts' because she was visibly pregnant. In just four months she would be delivered of the heir for which her husband had schemed so hard.

But the child born on 7 September that year turned out to be a girl. She was christened Elizabeth, and the pre-written letters announcing the birth made embarrassingly clear that this had not been the plan — a last-minute stroke of the pen had made the word 'Prince' into 'Princes[s]'. The jousting that had been organised to celebrate the new arrival was cancelled, and it was noted ominously that Henry did not attend the christening. Anne Boleyn might 'spurn our heads off like footballs', prophesied Thomas More, 'but it will not be long ere her head will dance the like dance'.

When Anne's second pregnancy ended in a miscarriage in January 1536 her fate was sealed, since Tudor medical science — or the lack of it — meant that one miscarriage might well be the first of an unbreakable series. This had been the case with Katherine, and once again Henry had not been slow in lining up a possible replacement for his non-productive Queen. He had set his cap at Jane Seymour, a soft-spoken young woman who was as meek and submissive as Anne had proved complicated and assertive.

Having made the Boleyn marriage possible, Thomas Cromwell was now given the job of destroying it. Anne had always been flirtatious, and this proved the route to her undoing. Playful glances and gestures were interpreted as evidence of actual infidelity. Men were tortured and 'confessions' produced. A court musician pleaded guilty to adultery. Her own brother was charged with incest. The facts were outlandish, but the servants of a Tudor government knew that 'proof' had to be found so that the defective Queen could be condemned. As Anne Boleyn prepared to step out on to Tower Green on 19 May 1536, the first Queen of England ever to be executed, she seemed to have reached her own peace. 'I hear the executioner is very good,' she said, 'and I have a little neck.' Then she put her hands around her throat and burst out laughing.

Henry wasted no time. No sooner had he received the news of Anne's beheading than he set off upriver on his barge to see Jane Seymour. Engaged the next day, the couple were married ten days later, and Jane was formally enthroned on Whit Sunday 4 June 1536 — in the very chair where Anne had sat only five weeks earlier.

From Henry's point of view, it was third time lucky. A kindly and level-headed woman in her late twenties, Jane worked hard to reconcile Henry with his elder daughter Mary, whose place in the succession he had given to Anne's daughter Elizabeth, and the lottery of fertility finally yielded the King the male heir that he wanted. At Hampton Court on 12 October 1537, Queen Jane was delivered of a healthy baby boy, whom Henry christened Edward, after the Confessor, the patron saint of English royalty. Henry at last had the token of divine blessing he had sought.

But his wife had suffered a disastrous delivery. According to one account, she had undergone the then primitive and almost invariably fatal surgery of a Caesarean section. Other evidence suggests blood poisoning of the placenta — puerperal fever. Either way, Prince Edward's mother died after twelve days of blood loss and infection that the royal doctors were helpless to reverse.

Henry was prostrated with unaccustomed sorrow. Jane Seymour lay in state for three weeks, and then, alone of Henry's wives, she was buried in pomp and glory in St George's Chapel at Windsor. It was later said that her name was on Henry's lips when he died, and certainly his will was to direct that he should be buried beside her. When the King of France sent his congratulations on the birth of a healthy heir, Henry's reply was uncharacteristically subdued. 'Divine Providence,' he wrote, 'hath mingled my joy with the bitterness of the death of her who brought me this happiness.'

Diplomatic dispatches are seldom to be taken at their face value, still less when worded by Henry VIII. But in this case we might, perhaps, give Henry the benefit of the doubt.

THE PILGRIMAGE OF GRACE

1536

EARLY-SIXTEENTH-CENTURY LIFE WAS INTER-woven with the joy of religious rite and spectacle — effigies of saints, stained-glass windows; the washing of feet on Maundy Thursday, the 'creeping to the cross' on Good Friday. In London every Whit Sunday, doves were released from the tower of St Paul's Cathedral to symbolise the Holy Spirit winging its way to heaven. This age-old texture of symbol and ritual provided a satisfying structure to most people's lives. The English were devout folk, reported one European traveller: 'they all attend mass every day'.

The miracle of the mass — the Holy Communion ser-vice when bread and wine were offered up at the altar —

was graphically described in Thomas Malory's *Morte D'Arthur*, the bestselling epic first printed and published by Caxton in 1485. As the bishop held up a wafer of bread, 'there came a figure in likeness of a child, and the visage was as red and as bright as any fire, and smote himself into the bread, that all they saw it that the bread was formed of a fleshly man'.

This was the moment of 'transubstantiation' when, according to Catholic belief, the bread and wine on the altar were literally transformed into the body and blood of Christ. It provided the awe-inspiring climax of every mass. Bells rang, incense wafted, and heads were bowed as Jesus himself, both child and 'fleshly man', descended from heaven to join that particular human congregation — to be devoured as the people ate his flesh and the priest alone drank his blood (the liquid that had once been wine was too precious to risk being passed around and spilled).

By the 1520s and 30s, the evangelical followers of Luther and Tyndale were openly scoffing at this potent but, to their mind, primitive and sacrilegious Catholic theatre. How could the Lord's sacred body be conjured up on earth by imperfect men in gaudy vestments? The exhilarating idea at the heart of the Reformation, that every man could have his own direct relationship with God, challenged the central role of the priest in religious ceremonies — and from this spiritual doubt followed material consequences. By what right did the clerics control their vast infrastructure of earthly power and possessions, notably the vast landed estates of the monasteries? The Church was by far the largest landowner in England.

In 1535 Henry VIII's chief minister, Thomas Cromwell,

seized on this appetising question: if the Church was corrupted by its involvement with worldly goods, why should he not relieve it of the problem? So he sent out his 'visitors', crews of inspectors who descended on the eight hundred or so monasteries and nunneries in England and duly discovered what they were sent to find. Laziness, greed and sexual peccadilloes: it was not difficult to unearth — or indeed, invent — evidence that some of the country's seven thousand monks, nuns and friars had been failing to live up to the high ideals they set themselves. Cromwell's inquisitors gleefully presented to their master plenty of examples of misconduct, along with some improbable relics — the clippings of St Edmund's toenails, St Thomas Becket's penknife. Their hastily gathered dossiers provided the excuse for the biggest land grab in English history, starting in 1536 with the dissolution of the smaller monasteries.

But the destruction of the country's age-old education, employment and social welfare network was not accomplished without protest. The monasteries represented everything that, for centuries, people had been taught to respect, and in October 1536 the north of England rose in revolt. Rallying behind dramatic banners depicting the five wounds of Christ, some forty thousand marchers came to the aid of Mother Church in a rebellion they proudly called the Pilgrimage of Grace.

The 'pilgrims' set about reinstating the monks and nuns in sixteen of the fifty-five houses that had already been suppressed. They demanded the legitimisation of Queen Katherine's daughter, Mary. They also called for the destruction of the disruptive books of Luther and Tyndale, and for the removal of Thomas Cromwell along with his ally Thomas Cranmer, the reforming Archbishop of Canterbury. The rebels had a fundamental faith in the orthodoxy of their monarch — if only King Henry's wicked advisers were removed, they believed, he would return to the good old ways.

This loyalty proved their undoing when Henry, unable to raise sufficient troops against them, bought time by agreeing to concede to the 'pilgrims' some of their demands; he invited their leader, Robert Aske, to come down to London and present his grievances in person, under safe conduct. But once the rebels were safely dispersed back home in their villages, Henry seized on the excuse of new risings in the early months of 1537 to exact revenge. 'Our pleasure,' he instructed his army commander, the Duke of Norfolk, '[is] that you shall cause such dreadful execution to be done upon a good number of every town village and hamlet that have offended as they may be a fearful spectacle to all others hereafter that would practise any like matter.'

Norfolk carried out his orders ruthlessly. Some seventy Cumberland villagers were hanged on trees in their gardens in full sight of their wives and children; the monks of Sawley, one of the monasteries reopened by the pilgrims, were hanged on long timber staves projecting from their steeple. Aske was executed in front of the people who had so enthusiastically cheered him a few months earlier.

The rebels had not been wrong in their hunch that Henry was at heart a traditional Catholic — the King believed in the miracle of transubstantiation to the day he died. Even as the Reformation progressed, he burned the reformers who dared to suggest that the bread and wine of the communion were mere symbols of Christ's body and blood. But he needed to fill his coffers. By 1540 England's last religious house, the rich Augustinian abbey of Waltham, had been closed and the royal treasury was richer by £132,000 (more than £50 million today) from the sale of the monastery lands.

Even richer in the long term were the squires, merchants and magnates who had been conscripted into the new order of things, picking up prime monastic acres all over the country. The Dissolution of the Monasteries was Henry's payoff to the landed classes, and it helped make the Reformation permanent.

But to this day we find corners of the English countryside curiously sanctified by the remains of high gothic arches, haunted towers and long-deserted cloisters. Rievaulx in north Yorkshire, Tintern in the Wye Valley, and Whitby on the windswept North Sea coast where St Hilda preached and the cowherd Caedmon sang: all these ghostly ruins are visible reminders of what was once the heart of English learning, education and history-making — a civilisation that consoled and inspired rich and poor alike for centuries.

. . . DIVORCED, BEHEADED, SURVIVED

1539‒47

IN THE SUMMER OF 1539 HENRY VIII STAGED a pageant on the River Thames. Two barges put out on to the water, one manned by a crew representing the King and his Council, the other by sailors in the scarlet costumes of the Pope and his cardinals. As Henry and crowds of Londoners looked on, the two boats met and engaged in mock battle, with much capering and horseplay until the inevitable happened — the scarlet-clad Pope and his cardinals were pitched into the river.

Real life was not so simple. In 1538 the Pope had issued a call to the Catholic powers of Europe to rally against England's 'most cruel and abominable tyrant' and England now found herself dangerously isolated. Thomas Cromwell's solution was to look for support among the Protestant princes of Germany. He could see how his royal master had been moping since the death of Jane Seymour a year or so earlier: perhaps business and pleasure could be combined by marriage to a comely German princess.

Inquiries established that there were two promising candidates in Cleves, the powerful north German duchy with its capital at Düsseldorf. The duke had a pair of marriageable sisters, Anne and Amelia, and early in 1539 Cromwell asked the English ambassador Christopher Mont to investigate their beauty. Mont reported back positively, and two locally produced portraits were sent off for the King's inspection. But were the likenesses trustworthy?

The answer was to dispatch the King's own painter, Hans Holbein, the talented German artist whose precise and luminous portraits embody for us the personalities and textures of Henry's court. Working quickly as usual, Holbein produced portraits of both sisters in little more than a week. That of Anne showed a serene and pleasant-looking woman, and legend has it that Henry fell in love with the portrait. In fact, the King had already decided that now, at forty-eight, he should go for the elder of the two sisters — the twenty-four-year-old Anne. The gentle, modest face that he saw in Holbein's canvas simply confirmed all the written reports he had received.

When Henry met his bride-to-be, however, he found her downright plain. 'I see nothing in this woman as men report of her,' he said, speaking 'very sadly and pensively' soon after he had greeted Anne on New Year's Day 1540. 'I marvel that wise men would make such report as they have done.'

Four days later Henry VIII went to his fourth marriage ceremony with a heavy heart. 'If it were not to satisfy the world and my realm,' he told Cromwell reproachfully on their way to the service, 'I would not do that I must do this day for none earthly thing.'

Next morning, Henry was in a thoroughly bad mood: there were still more grounds for reproach.

'Surely, as ye know,' he said to Cromwell, 'I liked her before not well, but now I like her much worse, for I have felt her belly and her breasts, and thereby, as I can judge, she should be no maid.' He added the indelicate detail that Anne suffered from bad body odour, and went on to describe the deflating effect this had on his ardour. 'I had neither will nor courage to proceed any further in other matters . . .' he confessed. 'I have left her as good a maid as I found her.'

The royal doctors were called in. It was a serious matter when a king could not consummate his marriage, but all they could offer was the age-old advice in such circumstances — not to worry too much. They advised Henry to take a night off.

But when the King returned to the fray, he found that nothing had changed — as Anne confirmed with charming innocence. 'When he comes to bed,' she told one of her ladies-in-waiting, 'he kisses me and taketh me by the hand and biddeth me "Goodnight, sweetheart". And in the morning [he] kisses me and biddeth me "Farewell, darling". Is this not enough?'

We know these extraordinary details because, not for the first time, Thomas Cromwell was allotted the task of undoing what he had done. A widely unpopular figure, he had pushed the reforming agenda too far for the tastes of many, and landing his master with a wife that Henry disparagingly called 'the Flanders Mare' proved the last straw. In June 1540 Cromwell became the latest of Henry's scapegoats, condemned for treason by act of Parliament and facing the dreadful penalties of hanging, drawing and quartering. If he wished to avoid this particular fate, the minister's final duty was to set down on paper the circumstantial evidence that would make possible the annulment of Henry's non-marriage to Anne.

Thomas Cromwell was executed — with an axe — on 28 July 1540; the paperwork he produced at the eleventh hour helped Henry secure annulment of the Cleves marriage. Just ten days later the King was married again, to Katherine Howard, the twenty-year-old niece of his fierce general in the north, the Duke of Norfolk. For nearly a year the traditionalist duke, a Catholic and a bitter enemy of Cromwell's, had been pushing the enticing Katherine into Henry's path while plotting his rival's downfall.

Unfortunately, the new Queen's lively allure was accompanied by a lively sexual appetite, and little more than a year after her marriage, rumours circulated about Katherine's promiscuity. As an unmarried girl in the unsupervised surroundings of the Norfolk household, she was said to have romped with Henry Manox her music teacher and also with her cousin Thomas Dereham — whom she then had the nerve to employ as her private secretary when she became Queen. In the autumn of 1541, during a royal progress to the north, inquiries revealed that she had waited till Henry was asleep before cavorting with another young lover, Thomas Culpeper.

Henry wept openly before his Council when finally confronted with proof of his wife's betrayal. Katherine was beheaded in February the next year, along with Culpeper, Manox the music teacher, her cousin Dereham and Lady Rochford, the lady-in-waiting who had facilitated the backstairs liaisons after the King had gone to sleep.

Henry was by now a gross and lumbering man-mountain, 'moved by engines and art rather than by nature', as the Duke of Norfolk put it. Arthritic and ulcerous, the ageing King had to be manhandled up staircases — a little cart was built to transport him around Hampton Court. His apothecary's accounts list dam-busting quantities of liquorice, rhubarb and other laxatives, along with grease for the royal haemorrhoids.

What Henry needed was a reliable and experienced wife, and he finally found one in Catherine Parr, thirty-one years old and twice widowed — which gave her the distinction of being England's most married Queen. In July 1543 she embarked sagely on the awesome challenge of life with England's most married king, bringing together his children Mary, Elizabeth and Edward to create, for the first time, something like a functional royal family household. Catherine was sympathetic to the new faith, and her most significant achievement, apart from surviving, was probably to en-sure that the two younger children, Edward and Elizabeth, were educated by tutors who favoured reform.

When Henry died on 28 January 1547, the news was kept secret for three days. It was difficult to imagine England without the lustful, self-indulgent tyrant who had once been the beautiful young sportsman-king. In moral terms the tale of his reign was one of remorseless decline, of power cor-rupting absolutely. By no measure of virtue could Henry VIII be called a good man.

But he was a great one — and arguably England's great-est ever king. Take virtue out of the equation, and his accom-plishments were formidable. He destroyed the centuries-old medieval Church. He revolutionised the ownership of En-glish land. He increased the power of central government to unprecedented heights, and though he ruled England as a despot, he did so without the support of an army. The new Church of England was Henry VIII's most obvious legacy. And in the turbulent years that followed his death the country's destiny would also be decisively shaped by the institution that he had enlisted — and thus, in the process, strengthened — to help him break from Rome: the Houses of Parliament and, in particular, the House of Commons.

BOY KING – EDWARD VI,
'THE GODLY IMP'

1547-53

AFTER ALL THE TROUBLE THAT HENRY VIII and England had gone through to get a male heir, Henry made sure that his son Edward received the best education that could be devised for a future king. The boy's tutors, Richard Cox and John Cheke, were the leading humanist scholars of the day, and they redoubled their efforts with the nine-year-old when he succeeded his father in January 1547. In his geography lessons Edward learned by heart the names of all the ports in England, Scotland and France, together with the prevailing winds and tides; in history he studied the long and disastrous reign of Henry VI, an object lesson in how *not* to rule. By the age of twelve, the 'godly imp' was reading twelve chapters of the Bible every day and taking notes as he listened to the Sunday sermon. In a display of cunning reminiscent of his grandfather Henry VII, the boy king devised his own secret code of Greek letters so no one could read his personal jottings.

Except for rejecting the authority of the Pope, Henry VIII had gone to his grave a pretty traditional Catholic. But he seems to have accepted that change must come: the two tutors he engaged for his son were prominent evangelicals, and he was well aware of the radical sympathies of his Archbishop of Canterbury Thomas Cranmer, who had been secretly preparing a programme of Protestant reform. For nearly twenty years Cranmer had hidden from his master the fact that he was married — Henry did not approve of married priests — but with Henry's death the archbishop's wife became public, and so did his programme of reform.

Out went the candles, the stained-glass windows, the statues of the Virgin and the colourful tableaux that had embellished the walls of the churches, which were now slapped over with a virtuous coat of whitewash. No more ashes on Ash Wednesday, no palms on Palm Sunday, and no creeping to the cross on Good Friday. Bells were pulled down from belfries, altar hangings and vestments were cut up to be used as saddle-cloths — and doves no longer flew from the tower of St Paul's on Whit Sunday. In just six years the changes were remarkable.

Today we delight in the beautiful and sonorous phrases of the Book of Common Prayer, first framed by Thomas

Cranmer in 1548-9, then revised in 1552. But this was a strange, discordant new language to the people of the time. While reformers obviously welcomed the change, they were in the minority. Most people felt themselves deprived of something they had known and loved all their lives.

Times were already unsettling enough. Inflation was rampant. By 1550, a silver penny contained a fifth of the silver content of 1500, having been so debased by the addition of red copper that, as Bishop Latimer put it, the coin literally 'blushed in shame'. Farming, the mainstay of the economy, was being transformed by rich landowners fencing in the common land. Large flocks of sheep, tended by a single shepherd boy, now grazed on pasture that had once supported half a dozen families ploughing their own strips.

These new fields, or 'enclosures', were helping enrich the Tudor squirearchy, but less affluent country-dwellers — the vast majority of the population — felt dispossessed. In the summer of 1549, villagers in East Anglia started uprooting hedges and seizing sheep by the thousand. They gathered on Mousehold Heath, outside Norwich, around a massive oak tree they called the Reformation Oak. Since Christ had died to make men free, they reasoned, they were demanding an end to bondage. In the West Country, the Cornish-speaking men of Cornwall had already risen in revolt, calling for the restoration of the mass in Latin, since they spoke little English. They had marched eastwards, besieging Exeter for thirty-five days.

Edward's tough councillors dealt with these and other risings in the traditional way — promising to listen to grievances, then meting out mortal punishment as soon as they had mustered their military strength. But inside his own family, Edward found a nut that could not be cracked. His elder sister Mary, thirty-two years old in January 1549, was an unashamed champion of the old faith, and she refused to prohibit the reading of the mass in her household as her brother requested. 'Death shall be more welcome to me,' she declared, 'than life with a troubled conscience.'

Edward's councillors tried for a compromise, but the boy king refused to give in on the matter. 'He would spend his life,' he said, 'and all he had, rather than agree and grant to what he knew certainly to be against the truth.'

His sister tried a mixture of flattery and condescension. 'Although your Majesty hath far more knowledge and greater gifts than others of your years, yet it is not possible that your Highness can at these years be a judge in matters of religion.'

Edward confirmed what a child he still was by breaking down in a fit of sobbing, 'his tender heart bursting out'. All the same, he refused to budge, as did Mary, who responded to his tears by repeating her willingness to be a martyr. 'Take away my life,' she said, 'rather than the old religion.'

This bitter clash between brother and sister showed that the obstinacy of Henry VIII lived on in both of them — as it did, for that matter, in their strong-willed half-sister Elizabeth, in 1553 approaching her twentieth birthday. It also suggested that the religious differences in their respective parentings might, in the future, cause turbulence and division. When Edward came down with a feverish cold in the spring of that year and could not shake it off, the whole pro-gramme of evangelical reform was suddenly in jeopardy. Ed-ward's Protestant advisers had no doubt that if the boy were to die and Mary succeed him, she would immediately set about dismantling all the changes they had put in place. En-gland would once again be subject to the Bishop of Rome. So what was to be done?

LADY JANE GREY —
THE NINE-DAY QUEEN

1553

A S THE FIFTEEN-YEAR-OLD EDWARD VI LAY sick at Greenwich in April and May 1553, his doctors were baffled by his 'weakness and faintness of spirit'. They noted a 'tough, strong, straining cough' — a possible sign of tuberculosis. Edward was coughing up blood; his body was covered with ulcers. In addition, there had been rumours that he was a victim of poison, so to protect themselves the doctors formally notified the Council that they feared the King had less than nine months to live.

On the death of Henry VIII, Edward's uncle Edward Seymour, Duke of Somerset, had taken charge of the boy king as 'Protector of the Realm'. Seymour was the elder brother of Henry's beloved third wife Jane, and it was under his auspices that the new Prayer Book of 1549 was introduced. But the risings of that year had marked the end of the Protector's power and provided an opening for John Dudley, son of Edmund Dudley, the overzealous fundraiser that Henry VIII had executed at the beginning of his reign.

His father's fate had not deterred John Dudley from the perilous path of Tudor royal service. In the autumn of 1549 his contribution to the crushing defeat of the Norfolk rebels at the Battle of Dussindale opened the way to him becoming Lord President of Edward's Council, and two years later he awarded himself the dukedom of Northumberland. With a boy king on the throne, the new duke was the effective ruler of England.

Yet Northumberland's power rested entirely on the fragile health of the real King, and as Edward sickened, the duke resorted to desperate measures. He persuaded the fevered young monarch to keep the throne from his Catholic sister by altering the succession in favour of Lady Jane Grey, Edward's cousin and great-granddaughter of Henry VII (see Tudor family tree, p. xi). Jane was intelligent and well educated, versed in Greek, Latin and Hebrew — and reliably Protestant. Born in October 1537, the same month as Edward, she had been brought up with him in the reform-minded household of Henry VIII's last Queen, Catherine Parr — Jane and Edward often attended the same lessons.

But the young woman's greatest attraction, from the Lord President's point of view, was that she offered a way of entrenching the Northumberlands in the royal succession. On 26 May 1553 the sixteen-year-old Lady Jane was married, against her will, to Northumberland's fourth son Guildford Dudley — her protests overruled by her father Henry Grey, Duke of Suffolk, who owed his elevated title to his old crony Northumberland.

Most of Northumberland's fellow-councillors were aghast at his naked grab for power. Archbishop Cranmer said he could not agree to the change until he had spoken personally with the King — but Edward, though drifting in and out of consciousness, was still set on denying England to Rome. He ordered Cranmer to endorse his Protestant cousin, and the archbishop reluctantly obeyed. The rest of the Council went along with him.

As letters patent were hastily drawn up declaring that Edward's two elder sisters Mary and Elizabeth were illegitimate, writs went out to summon a Parliament that would confirm the new succession. But the royal health was fast failing. By now Edward's digestion had ceased to function, and his hair and nails were dropping out. When he coughed he brought up foul-smelling black sputum. Death came, on 6 July, as a merciful release.

Two days earlier, Northumberland had summoned Princesses Mary and Elizabeth to their brother's deathbed. But Elizabeth declined the trap and Mary would move only cautiously. The moment the news of Edward's death reached her, she retired to Framlingham Castle in East Anglia and defiantly proclaimed her right to the throne. Down in London, meanwhile, Northumberland was proclaiming the new

Queen Jane. But as two heralds and a trumpeter made their way through the city, they met with a cold and indifferent response.

'No one present showed any sign of rejoicing,' reported one diplomat. When one herald cried, 'Long live the Queen', the only response came from the few archers who joined the sad trio.

In East Anglia it was equally clear where people's sympathies lay. Local gentlemen flocked to Framlingham with horsemen and retainers to pledge their loyalty to Mary. People who were unable to fight sent money or carts full of beer, bread and freshly slaughtered meat for the volunteer army, which by 19 July numbered nearly twenty thousand. When Mary rode out to thank them, she was greeted with 'shouts and acclamations' as men threw their helmets in the air. The noise frightened her horse so much she had to dismount and continue on foot through the mile-long encampment, greeting the soldiers personally and thanking them for their goodwill. Across the country there were enthusiastic demonstrations of support for Henry VIII's firstborn child, and local forces were quickly mustered.

It did not take long for the Council in London to get the message. Northumberland had headed north to arrest Mary, but his venture was clearly doomed. To save their own skins the colleagues he left in London, in a deft about-turn, offered a reward for his capture and proclaimed Mary's accession. In an explosion of popular joy people ran wild, crying out the news and dancing in the streets. As darkness fell, bonfires were lit. 'I am unable to describe to you,' wrote one visiting Italian,'nor would you believe the exultation of all men. From a distance the earth must have looked like Mount Etna.'

When Mary entered London on 3 August 1553, the celebrations knew no bounds. By then Northumberland had surrendered and had been sent to the Tower, where he was executed before the month was out. Lady Jane Grey was also imprisoned, but spared by Mary — she had clearly been only a pawn in the game.

Unfortunately for Jane, however, one of Mary's first decisions as Queen was to arrange a marriage for herself to the Catholic Philip of Spain. Early in 1554 the unpopularity of this 'Spanish match' prompted an uprising by Kentish rebels who reached the walls of London, and it became clear that the nine-day Queen, who embodied the hope for a Protestant succession, was too dangerous to be kept alive.

On 12 February 1554, Lady Jane Grey was led out to the block. It was some sort of poetic justice that along with her went Guildford Dudley, the husband she had not wished to marry, and Henry Grey, the father who had forced her into it.

BLOODY MARY AND THE
FIRES OF SMITHFIELD

1553-8

THE SPONTANEOUS REVOLT THAT PUT MARY
Tudor on the throne of England was the only popular
uprising to succeed in the 118 years of her dynasty's rule. '*Vox
Populi, Vox Dei*', read the banners that welcomed the daughter of Henry VIII and Katherine of Aragon to London in
the summer of 1553 — 'The voice of the people is the voice
of God.'

England had always felt sympathy, and perhaps a little
guilt, over the way that both Mary and her mother had been
treated during the break from Rome. Both women had stayed
true to their faith, and now the old religion was back. The al-

tars and vestments came out of hiding, and once again on feast days people could process and chant in church.

Mary believed in putting her intense personal piety into practice. She took the ceremonies of Maundy Thursday particularly seriously, covering her finery with a long linen apron to kneel in front of poor women, humbly washing, drying and kissing their feet. She would turn up at the door of needy households and of poor widows, in particular, dressed not as a queen but as a gentlewoman with offers of help. She liked to mingle with ordinary villagers, asking if they had enough to live on and, if they lived on royal estates, whether they were being fairly treated by the officers of the Crown. To judge by the folk tales told of Mary Tudor's charitable exploits, the Catholic Queen was a sixteenth-century combination of Mother Teresa and Diana, Princess of Wales.

But that is not, of course, how 'Bloody Mary' has been remembered by history, for there was a fanatical and unforgiving core to her faith. On 30 November 1554, the long and complicated legal process of reuniting the English Church with Rome was finally completed, with Parliament reinstating the medieval heresy statutes. If condemned by the church courts, heretics would now be handed over to the civil authorities to endure the grim penalty of burning to death at the stake. Less than three months later, the executions began.

Before the Reformation the public burning of heretics, which horrifies us today, was generally accepted — even popular. Since 1401, when the activities of the Lollards put burning on the Statute Book, the orthodox Catholic majority had felt strengthened in their own prospects for salvation by the sight of dissidents being reduced to ashes. Even as Henry VIII was breaking with Rome in the 1530s, his burning of especially vocal Protestants could be taken as demonstrating a sensible middle way. But by the 1550s the Protestants were no longer a crazy fringe. They made up a solid and respected minority of believers, and it was on them that Mary's zeal now focused.

From an early date, Mary's fervour worried those around her. In July 1554 she had provoked Protestant sensibilities by her marriage to the Catholic Philip of Spain — the Kent uprising that cost Lady Jane Grey her life only made Mary more determined — and even Philip's Spanish advisers counselled her against inflaming feelings further. But Mary felt she had compromised enough. Under pressure from her English councillors, many of them inherited from her brother Edward, she had reluctantly agreed to leave the monastery lands with those who had purchased them. But when it came to dogma, she had God's work to do. The burnings started in February 1555 with a selection of heretics both humble and mighty, among them the puritanical former Bishop of Gloucester, John Hooper.

Hooper was a victim of the local authorities' inexperience at the practicalities of this rare and specialised form of execution. They had supplied only two saddle-loads of reeds and faggots — and because the wood was green it burned slowly. Hooper desperately clasped bundles of reeds to his chest in a vain attempt to hasten the process, but only the bottom half of his body was burning. 'For God's love, good people,' he cried out, 'let me have more fire!'

In these early days the burnings were well attended. For the citizens of Gloucester there was a novelty value, and perhaps even a ghoulish attraction, in watching their once high-and-mighty bishop agonise in front of their eyes. But the very suffering began to alter opinion — the smell of burning human flesh turns even the strongest stomach — and the executions of Bishops Hugh Latimer and Nicholas Ridley at Oxford on 16 October that same year came to symbolise the tragedy of good men being tortured for their sincere beliefs.

Ridley had been Bishop of London and had played a major role in drafting the Book of Common Prayer of 1549. Latimer was a populist preacher well known for his sympathy for the poor. Famous for blending theology with everyday social concerns in open-air sermons that he delivered to large crowds, he had proudly refused the escape route that many radicals took to the German states and Swiss cities where Protestants were safe. As he and Ridley were being trussed to the same stake, he uttered the words that would forever evoke Mary's martyrs: 'Be of good comfort, Master Ridley, and play the man; we shall this day, by God's grace, light such a candle in England as I trust shall never be put out.'

Though Latimer died quite quickly, suffocated by the smoke and losing consciousness, the fire burned more slowly on Ridley's side. As was becoming the custom, his family had bribed the executioner to tie a bag of gunpowder around his neck, but the flames were not reaching high enough to trigger this ghastly if merciful release. 'I cannot burn,' Ridley cried, screaming in pain until a guard pulled away some of the damp faggots. Immediately the flames leapt upwards, and as Ridley swung his head down towards them the gunpowder exploded.

Watching this excruciating agony was the former Archbishop of Canterbury, Thomas Cranmer. The Catholic authorities were trying to terrify him into recanting his faith — and they succeeded. Under the pressures of prison life, constant hectoring and sheer fear, Cranmer signed no less than six recantations, each more abject than the one before. The great architect of England's Protestant Reformation was even driven to accept the Catholic doctrine of transubstantiation and the authority of the Pope.

But Cranmer still was not spared. Mary's determination to punish the archbishop who had annulled her mother's marriage and proclaimed her a bastard was unassailable. His burning was set for 21 March 1556, on the same spot in Oxford where Ridley and Latimer had died, and he was led into the university church to pronounce his final, public recantation.

But having embarked on the preamble that the authorities were expecting, Cranmer suddenly changed course. He wished to address, he said, 'the great thing which so much troubleth my conscience', and he began to explain that the recantations he had signed were 'contrary to the truth which I thought in my heart'. As uproar broke out in the church, he raised his voice to a shout: 'As for the Pope, I refuse him, as Christ's enemy and Antichrist!'

The white-bearded ex-archbishop was dragged out and hurried to the stake, where fire was put to the wood without delay. As the flames licked around him, he extended towards them the 'unworthy right hand' with which he had signed his recantations.

Cranmer's death was a propaganda disaster for Mary's government. Even loyal Catholics could see the unfairness in someone who had repeatedly recanted being punished just the same. In the forty-five killing months between 4 February 1555 and 10 November 1558, 283 martyrs — 227 men and 56 women — were burned alive for their faith. By June of that final year Londoners were reacting with anger and distaste: the burnings, hitherto held in front of St Bartholomew's Hospital in Smithfield, had to be shifted to secret places of execution. And elsewhere, things were looking no better for Henry VIII's eldest child. Earlier in 1558 her armies had been driven out of the fortified port of Calais, the last vestige of England's empire across the Channel; and she herself was mortally ill, dying of a stomach tumour that she had imagined to be a baby that would keep the Catholic cause alive.

The very opposite proved the case — for the reign which began with such popular promise ended by inspiring a hostility to 'popery' in England that is embedded to this day. It is still impossible for a British king or queen to be Roman Catholic or to marry a Roman Catholic, and the roots of the bitter hatreds that divide Northern Ireland can be similarly traced back to the fires of Smithfield. Stubborn, pious, Catholic Mary had helped make England a Protestant nation.

ROBERT RECORDE AND HIS
INTELLIGENCE SHARPENER

1557

ROBERT RECORDE WAS A WELSHMAN WHO studied at both Oxford and Cambridge in the reign of Henry VIII, before moving down to London to work as a doctor — he was consulted, on occasion, by both Edward VI and Mary. But it is for his maths that he is remembered. In 1543 he published *The Ground of Arts*, the first ever maths book in English, which ran through over fifty editions and introduced English schoolchildren to the tortured delights of such problems as: 'If a horse has four shoes, each with six nails, and you pay half a penny for the first nail, one penny for the second, two for the third, four for the fourth, and so on, doubling every time, how much will the shoeing of the horse cost?'

The modern historian Adam Hart-Davis has pointed out that there are, in fact, two answers to this problem: 126 pence, if the shoes are counted separately — that is, 4 lots of 6 nails — or 8,388,607.5 pence (£34,952) if you continue the doubling process as you move through all the shoes and nails.

In 1556, in *The Castle of Knowledge*, Recorde set out some of the revolutionary ideas of the Polish astronomer Nicolaus Copernicus who had died in 1543. After a lifetime of studying the stars, Copernicus had come to the conclusion that the earth is *not* the centre of the universe, but moves around the sun, while also spinning on its own axis. Copernicus had been careful to keep his heretical observations to himself in his lifetime — it was an article of Catholic faith that the heavens moved around God's earth — and Recorde, writing in the reign of Bloody Mary, exercised similar prudence: 'I will let it pass till some other time,' he wrote.

But the innovation for which the Welshman is remembered today appeared the following year in his algebra book, *The Whetstone of Wit* ('The Intelligence Sharpener'). Until 1557, mathematicians had finished off a calculation by laboriously writing out the words '. . . is equal to . . .', which was sometimes abbreviated to *ae* (or *oe*), from the Latin word for equal — *aequalis*. But Recorde had a better idea: why not use a symbol? 'To avoide the tedious repetition of these woords', he proposed the use of a pair of parallel lines: =.

Using the simple device that we now call 'the equals sign' released an enormous log jam in the efficient handling of numbers, and the implications extended far beyond pure maths. It immensely speeded up the calculations of astronomers and navigators — even shopkeepers — and what could be more satisfying for everyone than to round off a calculation with two elegant little parallel lines? As Recorde himself put it — 'noe two things can be moare equalle'.

ELIZABETH — QUEEN OF HEARTS

1559

ELIZABETH I WAS CROWNED IN WESTMINSTER Abbey on 15 January 1559 — a date selected by her astrologer, Dr John Dee. Cheering crowds had lined the route as she set off from the City of London the previous day, and the red-haired Queen had time for everyone, holding hands, cracking jokes and watching with rapt attention the loyal pageants staged in her honour. When the figure of Truth approached her, carrying a Bible, the twenty-five-year-old monarch kissed the holy book fervently and clasped it to her breast.

Flamboyant and theatrical, Elizabeth was very much her father's daughter — with the dash and temper (as well as the piercing dark eyes) of her mother Anne Boleyn. Tudor to the core, she was spiky, vain and bloody-minded, with the distrustfulness of her grandfather Henry VII whose penny-pinching she also matched. At the receiving end of arbitrary power during her youth, she had lived with rejection and danger and survived to boast about it. 'I thank God,' she told her Members of Parliament a few years after she came to power, 'that I am endued with such qualities that if I were turned out of the Realm in my petticoat, I were able to live in any place in Christendom.'

On the first day of her reign, the new Queen selected as her principal adviser William Cecil, her efficient estate manager whom she liked to call her 'spirit'. In fact, this hardworking servant of the Crown was anything but airy-fairy — Cecil provided ballast to the royal flightiness. At nine o'clock on the dot, three mornings a week, the dry little secretary summoned the Council to plough through the detail of administration. One early reform was to call in the much-debased 'pink' silver pennies for re-minting: within two years the coinage was so well re-established that the government actually made a profit. Her reign also saw the creation of England's first stock exchange. And to build up the nation's shipping capacity — as well as its seafarers — it became compulsory in Elizabeth's England to eat fish on Wednesdays and Saturdays.

But it was religion that was the priority after the trauma of Mary's excesses. Traditionally minded, like her father, Elizabeth favoured beautiful vestments, crucifixes and candlesticks, insisting there should be ceremony at the heart of Sunday worship. Also like her father, she disliked the newfangled Protestant notion of allowing the clergy to marry, and made clear her disapproval of their wives. England's Catholics were also reassured when she declined to reclaim her father's title as Supreme Head of the Church. It was a subtle distinction, but she settled for Supreme Governor.

For their part, Protestants were pleased to see the powerful rhythms of Cranmer's Book of Common Prayer restored, and hear again William Tyndale's robust English ringing out when the gospel was read. Elizabeth offered both sides a compromise, and she promised no trouble to those who would live and let live — she did not wish to make, in Francis Bacon's words, 'windows into men's souls'. Elizabeth's attempt at a tolerant middle way came to define a certain strand of Englishness.

One subject on which she disagreed, however, with virtually every man in England — including William Cecil — was on her need to take a husband. It was inconceivable in the sixteenth century that a woman could lead a proper life, let alone run a country, without a better half: in 1566, in a telling display of insubordination, Parliament threatened to refuse to levy taxes unless the Queen took a husband. But Elizabeth was only too aware that if she married a foreign prince England would get embroiled in European wars, while an English husband could not help but provoke domestic jealousies. 'I am already bound to a husband,' she liked to say, 'which is the kingdom of England.'

Thus came into being the powerful myth of Gloriana the Virgin Queen — bedecked in jewels and an endless succession of spectacular dresses that took on the status of semi-sacred vestments. Homage to this stylised, white-faced icon became compulsory — a draft proclamation of 1563 sought to insist that all portraits of Elizabeth had to be copied from one approved template. When John Stubbs, an evangelical pamphleteer, dared to criticise the Queen's marriage policy in 1579, he was sentenced to have his writing hand chopped off with a cleaver. 'God save the Queen!' he cried out after his right hand was severed, raising his hat with his left.

This tyrannical, capricious monarch was the inspiration for the most glittering and creative court England has ever seen. Every year Elizabeth would embark on her 'progresses' — glorified summer holidays — in which the Queen, accompanied by her court and by a veritable army of horses and carts, set off to cadge free hospitality from the great of the land in their magnificent new windowed country houses.

Well before the end of the century, Elizabeth's accession day, 17 November, had come to be celebrated as a national holiday. Bells would be rung, toasts drunk, and poems composed in praise of the Faerie Queen who had made herself the embodiment of a dynamic and thrusting nation. And if by the end of the century the physical reality of Elizabeth in her sixties, lined and black-toothed, scarcely matched the idealised prints and portraits of the young monarch she once had been, people willingly suspended disbelief.

In 1601 she received a deputation from the House of Commons, furious at the many abuses and shortcomings of her government in these her declining years. But when, bewigged, bejewelled and beruffed, she responded to them directly yet again, they fell willingly under her spell. 'Though God has raised me high,' she declaimed, in what became known as her 'Golden Speech', 'yet this I count the glory of my crown, that I have reigned with your loves . . . Though you have had and may have many mightier and wiser princes sitting on this seat, yet you never had nor shall have any that will love you better.' The frail and fractious old lady was sixty-seven years old. But to her listeners she remained Gloriana, and one by one they shuffled forward to kiss her hand.

THAT'S ENTERTAINMENT

1571

A S YOU APPROACHED QUEEN ELIZABETH'S
London from the south you were confronted by a
ghastly sight. Down from the stone gateway above London
Bridge grimaced a row of rotting and weathered skulls —
the severed heads of traitors, some of them generations
old. Every sixteenth-century town had its hanging place, a
purpose-built gallows or a tree where malefactors were executed and left to putrefy, dangling there as a warning to others. There were several gallows in London. Twenty to thirty
offenders were hanged every day the law courts sat, reported
one Swiss-German traveller in 1599, who was clearly rather
impressed.

In a field to the west of London stood Tyburn Tree, the capital's busiest hanging place — and hence a major venue for popular entertainment, where rowdy crowds gathered and children, straining to get a glimpse, would be hoisted on to their parents' shoulders to cheer and jeer. Food and drink stalls did a brisk trade in pies, fruit and sweetmeats at the spot that is marked today by an iron plaque in the middle of the traffic island, near Speakers' Corner, just across from the fast food and takeaway shops of Marble Arch.

By 1571 the gallows traffic was such that a large wooden contraption had to be built on which as many as twenty-four bodies could be strung at once. The executioner was a local butcher who would tie a rope round the criminal's neck while he sat in a cart. When the cart moved on, the victim was left dangling, and his friends ran forward to hang on his legs and try to hasten his painful strangulation. In 1577 the topographer-chronologist William Harrison's *Description of England* listed the hanging crimes as buggery, murder, manslaughter, treason, rape, felony, hawk-stealing, witchcraft, desertion in the field of battle, highway robbery and the malicious letting-out of ponds.

Many Elizabethan amusements were brutal by our tastes. In 1562 an Italian visitor, Alessandro Magno, described a Sunday-afternoon session at one of London's animal-baiting pits, where admission cost the modern equivalent of £2 for standing room and £4 for a seat:

> *First they take into the ring a cheap horse . . . and a monkey in the saddle. Then they attack the horse with 5 or 6 of the youngest dogs. Then they change the dogs for more experienced ones . . . It*

is wonderful to see the horse galloping along . . . with the monkey holding on tightly to the saddle and crying out frequently when he is bitten by the dogs. After they have entertained the audience for a while with this sport, which often results in the death of the horse, they lead him out and bring in bears — sometimes one at a time, sometimes all together. But this sport is not very pleasant to watch. At the end, they bring on a fierce bull and tie it with a rope about two paces long to a stake fixed in the middle of the ring. This sport is the best one to see, and more dangerous for the dogs than the others: many of them are wounded and die. This goes on until evening.

It is a relief to turn to descriptions of the innovative wooden structures that were being built among the bear-pits of Southwark — the playhouses. In the early Tudor decades, pageants and rudimentary plays had been performed in tavern courtyards and in noble households by touring companies of players. But 1587 saw the construction of England's first modern theatre, the Rose, an open-air stage and arena surrounded by wooden galleries — an enlarged and exalted version, in effect, of the tavern courtyard. 'They play on a raised platform,' wrote the Swiss traveller Thomas Platter, 'so that everyone has a good view. There are different galleries and places, however, where the seating is better and more comfortable and therefore more expensive . . . During the performance food and drink are carried round the audience . . . The actors are most expensively and elaborately costumed.'

Today one can get a taste of Elizabethan theatregoing by visiting the Globe, a modern reconstruction of the original theatre that opened in Southwark in January 1599. By that date there was a little clutch of playhouses on the south bank of the Thames, safely outside the jurisdiction of London's City Fathers, who disapproved of the low and licentious shows that tempted people away from work in the afternoons. The best-designed playhouses faced south-west so they could catch the afternoon sun as it set; the outstanding productions were honoured by an invitation to go and perform at court in the presence of Elizabeth.

William Shakespeare is the most famous of an entire school of English playwrights who were the equivalent of the TV programme makers of today, churning out soap operas, thrillers, comedies and even multi-part series: we watch docudramas on the world wars and on twentieth-century history — the Elizabethans sat through *Henry VI Parts 1, 2 and 3*. To appeal to the groundlings in the pit, the playwrights wrote slapstick comedies at which the Queen herself was known to slap a thigh — Shakespeare's most farcical play, *The Merry Wives of Windsor*, was written at her request. But they also invented a new dramatic form — the introspective soliloquy that showed how a harsh age was also becoming reflective and questioning: 'To be, or not to be — that is the question . . .'

SIR WALTER RALEGH AND
THE LOST COLONY

1585

WALTER RALEGH WAS A SWAGGERING West Country lad who started his career as a soldier of fortune. He was only sixteen when he crossed the Channel to fight on the side of the Huguenots, the French Protestants, in the religious wars that divided France for much of the sixteenth century. Later he fought against the Catholics in Ireland.

Ralegh was six feet tall by the time he came to court in the late 1570s, handsome and well built, with a jutting chin and dark curling hair shown off to perfection with a double pearl drop-earring. He has gone down in history for his rich and flashy clothes, and for many twentieth-century British schoolchildren the name Ralegh (or Raleigh — the 'i' was added in later years) stood for sturdy bicycles and for cloaks in the mud:

> *This Captain Ralegh, [runs the earliest version of the famous story] coming out of Ireland to the English court in good habit — his clothes being then a considerable part of his estate — found the Queen walking, till, meeting with a plashy place, she seemed to scruple going thereon. Presently Ralegh cast and spread his new plush cloak on the ground; whereon the Queen trod gently over, rewarding him afterwards with many suits for his so free and seasonable tender of so fair a foot cloth.*

This gallant tale was not recorded for another eighty years, but something like it almost certainly happened: one version of Ralegh's coat of arms featured a visual pun on the story — a plush and swirling cloak. Sir Walter epitomised the peacockery that danced attendance on the Virgin Queen, and Elizabeth was entranced by the style with which he played her game. She made him her Captain of the Guard. She liked 'proper men' and Ralegh was certainly one of those — though, not quite properly, 'he spake broad Devonshire till his dying day'.

As a West Countryman, Ralegh made himself the champion at court for the growing number of Elizabethans who were drawn towards the New World. Among these were relatives like his half-brother Humphrey Gilbert, who vanished in 1583 while searching for a route that would lead him to the riches of China through the ice floes and mist-laden inlets that lay beyond Newfoundland — the 'North West

Passage'. Adventurers such as Francis Drake and Richard Grenville saw good Protestant duty, as well as piracy and plunder, in capturing Spanish galleons and challenging the Catholic King of Spain (who after 1581 also took over Portugal and its colonies). The guru of the New World enthusiasts was Dr John Dee, the Merlin-like figure who had cast the Queen's coronation horoscope. Dee put forward the ambitious idea of a 'British Impire' across the Atlantic — a land first discovered, he said, not by John Cabot in 1497 but by Madoc, a Welsh prince in the King Arthur mould, who was said to have crossed the Atlantic centuries previously.

In the early 1580s Dee provided Ralegh with a map of the American coastline north of Florida. Ralegh dispatched scouts to search for a suitable settlement, and in 1585 he presented the results of their prospecting to Elizabeth — two native Indians, some potatoes, and the curious leaf smoked by the natives: tobacco.

The Elizabethans considered the potato an exotic and aphrodisiac vegetable. When Sir John Falstaff was attempting to have his wicked way with the merry wives of Windsor, he called on the sky to 'rain potatoes'. As for tobacco, the 'herb' was considered a health-giving medicine, which 'purgeth superfluous phlegm and other gross humours and openeth all the pores and passages of the body'.

Sir John Hawkins had introduced tobacco to England twenty years earlier, but it was typical of Ralegh to hijack the brand identity with a stunt to match the cloak and puddle. Talking to the Queen one day he boasted he could weigh tobacco smoke. Not surprisingly, Elizabeth challenged him, and he called for scales. Having weighed some tobacco, he smoked it in his long-stemmed pipe, then weighed the ashes and calculated the difference. As a final flourish, he proposed that the land where this remarkable plant grew should be named in her honour — Virginia.

Ralegh's prospective colonists set sail for the New World in May 1587 — ninety men, seventeen women and nine children — with all the supplies they needed to establish a self-sustaining and civilised community, including books, maps, pictures and a ceremonial suit of armour for John White, who was to be the governor. They landed on the island of Roanoke off modern North Carolina, and established what seemed to be relatively friendly relations with the local Croatoan Indians. But only a month after landing it became clear that more supplies would be needed, so Governor White set sail to organise a relief expedition for the following spring.

But White arrived home to find England transfixed by the threat of Spanish invasion. Though chief promoter of the Virginia colony, Ralegh had not sailed himself with his adventurers, and now he was tied up organising ships to combat the threat of King Philip's Armada. There was not a vessel to be spared, so it was August 1590 before Governor White could finally drop anchor off Roanoke again — nearly three years after he had departed. To his delight he saw smoke rising from the island, but when he landed he discovered it was only a forest fire. There was no trace of the colonists.

'We let fall our grapnel near the shore,' White related poignantly, 'and sounded with a trumpet and call, and afterwards many familiar English tunes of songs, and called to them friendly. But we had no answer.'

Locating the ruins of the palisade and cabins that he had helped to build, White discovered only grass, weeds and pumpkin creepers. But there were fresh native footprints in the sand — and one sign of Western habitation: a post on which were carved the letters, 'CROATOAN'. White had agreed with the colonists that if they moved to a new settlement, they would leave its name carved somewhere on Roanoke. But when he investigated the nearby Croatoan Island, he found no sign of human habitation.

In later years archaeologists and historians would search for evidence of what might have happened to Walter Ralegh's 'lost colony'. Recent diggings have uncovered the English fort and what appears from the assembled samples of flora and fauna to be a primitive science and research centre, North America's first. But the only clue to what happened to the colonists — and that is tenuous — has been found in modern Robertson County in North Carolina. Survivors of an Indian tribe there, called the Croatoans, speak a dialect containing words that sound a little like Elizabethan English — and some of these modern Croatoans have fair skin and blue eyes.

MARY QUEEN OF SCOTS

1560-87

WHEN IT CAME TO DEALING WITH THE other kingdom that occupied their island, English monarchs sometimes sent armies north of the border, and sometimes brides. Henry VII's daughter Margaret Tudor had been the last bridal export — she had married James Stuart, King of the Scots, in 1503 (see p. 78), and her glamorous but troubled granddaughter Mary was to provide Elizabeth I with the longest-running drama of her reign.

Mary's life was dramatic from the start. Her father James V of Scotland died when she was only six days old — and for the rest of her life she bore her famous title Queen of Scots. She was Queen of France too for a time, thanks to her brief first marriage to the French King François II. But François died in 1560, and his eighteen-year-old widow returned to the turmoil of the Scottish Reformation.

The young Queen was not well received by John Knox, the fiery leader of Scotland's evangelicals, who had just published his virulent denunciation of female rulers, *The First Blast of the Trumpet against the Monstrous Regiment of Women*. Mary's Catholicism was another black mark against her in Knox's eyes, and as Protestantism became the official religion of Scotland in the early 1560s she had to pick her way carefully, prudently confining her beliefs to her own household.

But after several years of delicate and quite skilful balancing, Mary succumbed to the first of the headstrong impulses that would turn her promising young life to tragedy. In July 1565, she plunged into a passionate marriage with her cousin Henry Stuart, Lord Darnley, whose good looks masked a vain, drunken, jealous and violent nature — as he proved within months, when he arranged for a gang of cronies to set upon Mary's Italian private secretary, David Rizzio. Darnley's possessiveness could not tolerate the trust that his wife placed in her chief of staff, and as the hapless Italian clung screaming to the Queen's skirts — she was now six months pregnant — he was murdered in front of her eyes.

Compared to the canniness with which her English cousin Elizabeth steered clear of marital entanglement, Mary was worse than impulsive: she was self-destructive. Within a year of Rizzio's murder she was romantically involved with another homicidal aristocrat, James, Earl of Bothwell, who devised nothing less than the blowing-up of the bedridden Darnley who, after a youth of debauchery, had been laid low by the ravages of syphilis. Mary herself may even have been complicit in the murder. She had spent the evening of 10 February 1567 visiting her ailing husband in his house at Kirk o' Field, Edinburgh, before leaving for Holyrood Palace between ten and eleven o'clock. Two hours after midnight all Edinburgh was rocked as the house exploded. Darnley's lifeless body was found in the garden.

Mary's marriage to Bothwell only three months later confirmed Scottish suspicions of her involvement, and ended her last chance of being a credible ruler. In July that year she was compelled to abdicate in favour of her thirteen-month-old son James (Darnley's child), and in May 1568 at the age of twenty-five she fled from Scotland in disgrace to throw herself on the mercy of her cousin Elizabeth.

Elizabeth had been viewing Mary's melodramatic adventures across the border with fascination — and not a little rivalry. Nine years younger than Elizabeth, Mary was generally reckoned a beauty, and this piqued the jealousy of the English Queen. In 1564 she had cornered the Scottish ambassador Sir James Melville, putting his diplomacy to the test as she cross-questioned him on the looks of his Scottish mistress. Elizabeth got crosser and crosser as Melville dodged her traps — until he let slip that Mary was taller. 'Then she is too high,' exclaimed Gloriana in triumph. 'I myself am neither too high, nor too low!'

Mary's arrival as an uninvited asylum seeker placed Elizabeth in a dilemma. England could hardly provide money, still less an army, to restore the deposed Queen — this would impose an unpopular Catholic monarch on Scotland's staunch Protestants. But since blood made Mary next in line to Elizabeth's own throne, she could not, either, be allowed to leave England lest she fall into the clutches of France or Spain. The Queen of Scots would have to be kept in some kind of limbo.

To start with, the fiction was maintained that Mary, as a cousin and anointed monarch, was being received in England as Elizabeth's honoured guest. Yet Elizabeth did not visit Mary — the two women never met — and as the Queen of Scots was shifted across the north of England from one residence to another, it became clear that she was under house arrest. With a bodyguard that was curiously large for a cousin who was supposed to be trusty and beloved, Mary was shuttled from Carlisle to Bolton, then on to Tutbury in Staffordshire.

The transfer that made her captivity plain occurred late in 1569, when the Catholics of the north rose in revolt. As the rebels burned the English prayer books and Bibles, restoring church altars so as to celebrate the Roman mass in all its splendour, the earls who headed the rising dispatched a kidnap squad to Tutbury. Only in the nick of time did William Cecil have Mary whisked southwards to the fortified walls of the city of Coventry, and though the revolt collapsed, the Queen of Scots was now clearly identified as the focus of Catholic hopes. In February 1570, Pope Pius V formally excommunicated Elizabeth and called on all Catholics to rise up, depose and, if necessary, murder the 'heretic Queen'.

The papal decree was to become Mary's death sentence, but Elizabeth could not bring herself to go along with the simple but ruthless solution proposed by her anxious councillors, and particularly by her spymaster Sir Francis

Walsingham — England would not be safe, in their opinion, until the Queen of Scots was dead. In the meantime, the bodyguards kept moving Mary onwards — from Coventry to Chatsworth, then on to Sheffield, Buxton, Chartley, and finally to Fotheringhay Castle in Rutland, now Northamptonshire. As she travelled, Walsingham's network of secret agents kept working to entrap her and, after a decade and a half, in October 1586 they had finally secured the evidence they required.

Imprudently, Mary had been plotting with fellow-Catholics through coded letters smuggled in waterproof pouches hidden in beer casks. But the whole scheme was of Walsingham's invention — a sting devised to incriminate Mary — and when she was put on trial at Fotheringhay it was revealed that his cipher clerks had been decoding her messages within hours of her sending them off.

Mary Queen of Scots was found guilty of treason and sentenced to death on 4 December that year. But again Elizabeth hesitated, and for weeks she could not bring herself to sign the death warrant — and then only in a contradictory fashion, first ordering her secretary William Davison to seal it, then instructing that it should not be sealed until further ordered. It was her councillors who took matters into their own hands by sealing the warrant and sending it north without informing the Queen.

On 8 February 1587, in the great hall at Fotheringhay, Mary went to the block with dignity, dressed dramatically in a blood-red shift, her eyes blindfolded with a white silk cloth. She was praying as the axe descended, and as the second blow severed her head, some witnesses maintained they could see her lips still moving in silent prayer.

'God save the Queen!' cried the executioner — but as he reached down to grasp Mary's head, her auburn hair came off in his hands: her wigless, grey-stubbled head fell to the ground and rolled unceremoniously across it.

Down in London, Elizabeth threw a fit of sorrow, surprise and anger at the death of her royal cousin. She raged at the councillors who had sent off the warrant without her final authority. She dispatched Secretary Davison to the Tower for eighteen months, and he was never restored to royal favour. When it came to necessary brutalities, Gloriana was as skilled at finding scapegoats as her father Henry VIII.

SIR FRANCIS DRAKE AND THE SPANISH ARMADA

1588

IN ENGLAND HIS NAME DESCRIBED A MALE waterfowl that might be seen bobbing placidly on the village pond — but in Spanish the drake became a dragon. El Draque was a name with which to frighten naughty children, a fire-breathing monster whose steely, glittering scales 'remained impregnable', wrote the sixteenth-century dramatist Lope de Vega, 'to all the spears and all the darts of Spain'.

By the 1580s, Francis Drake's reputation provoked panic in the seaports of Spain and in its New World colonies. In a series of daring raids, the rotund Devon-born pirate had pillaged Spanish harbours, looted Catholic churches and hijacked King Philip's silver bullion as it travelled from the mines of the Andes to the Spanish treasury in Seville. In his most famous exploit, during 1577-80, Drake had sailed round the world claiming California for Queen Elizabeth and arriving home laden with treasure. No wonder she knighted him — and that his ship the *Golden Hind*, moored at Deptford near London, became the tourist attraction of the day.

Now, on 20 July 1588, Sir Francis was taking his ease at Plymouth with the other commanders of the English navy, preparing to confront the great war fleet — *armada* in Spanish — that Philip II had marshalled to punish the English for their piracy and Protestantism. According to the chronicler John Stow, writing a dozen years after the event, the English officers were dancing and revelling on the shore as the Spanish Armada hove into sight.

It was not until 1736, 148 years later, that the famous tale was published of how Drake insisted on finishing his game of bowls before he went to join his ship. But the story could well be true. The tide conditions were such on that day in 1588 that it was not possible to sail out of Plymouth Sound until the evening, and the Spanish ships were scarcely moving fast. Indeed, their speed has been calculated at a stately walking pace — just two miles an hour — as they moved eastwards in a vast crescent, heading for the Straits of Dover, then for the Low Countries, where they were planning to link up with the Duke of Parma and his army of invasion.

According to folklore, the Spanish galleons were massive and lumbering castles of the sea that towered over the vessels of the English fleet. In fact, the records show the chief fighting ships on both sides to have been of roughly similar size — about a thousand tons. The difference lay in the ships' designs, for while the English galleons were sleek and nippy, custom-made for piracy and for manoeuvring in coastal waters, the Spanish ships were full-bellied, built for steadiness as they transported their cargo on the long transatlantic run.

More significantly, the English ships carried twice the cannon power of their enemies', thanks, in no small part, to the zeal of Henry VIII. Elizabeth's polymath father had taken an interest in artillery, encouraging a new gun-building technology developed from bell-founding techniques: in 1588 some of the older English cannon that blasted out at the Spanish galleons had been recast from the copper and tin alloy melted down from the bells of the dissolved monasteries.

Popular history has assigned Francis Drake the credit for defeating the Spanish Armada. In fact, Drake almost scuppered the enterprise on the very first night: he broke formation to go off and seize a disabled Spanish vessel for himself. The overall commander of the fleet was Lord Howard of Effingham, and it was his steady strategy to keep pushing the Spanish up the Channel, harrying them as they went. 'Their force is wonderful great and strong,' wrote Howard to Elizabeth on the evening of 29 July, 'and yet we pluck their feathers by little and little.'

Ashore in England, meanwhile, the beacons had been lit. A chain of hilltop bonfires had spread the news of the Armada's sighting, and the militia rallied for the defence of the shires. Lit today to celebrate coronations and royal jubilees, this network of 'fires over England' dated back to medieval times. Seventeen thousand men rapidly mustered in the south-east, and early in August Queen Elizabeth travelled to inspect them at Tilbury as they drilled in preparation for confronting Parma's invasion force. According to one account, the fifty-four-year-old Queen strapped on a breastplate herself to deliver the most famous of the well-worded speeches that have gilded her reputation:

> *I am come amongst you, as you see . . . in the midst and heat of the battle, to live and die amongst you all . . . I know I have the body of a weak and feeble woman, but I have the heart and the stomach of a king, and a king of England too, and think it foul scorn that Parma, or Spain, or any prince of Europe should dare to invade the borders of my realm . . . We shall shortly have a famous victory over those enemies of my God, my kingdom and my people.*

By the time Elizabeth delivered this speech, on 9 August 1588, the famous victory had already been won. Several nights previously, Howard had dispatched fire ships into the Spanish fleet as it lay at anchor off the Flanders coast, and in the resulting confusion the Spanish had headed north, abandoning their rendezvous with Parma. Fleeing in front of their English pursuers, they took the long way home, heading round the top of Scotland and Ireland. Almost half the Armada, including many of the best warships, managed to make it back to Spain. But over eleven thousand Spaniards perished, and the great crusade to which the Pope and several Catholic nations had contributed ended in humiliation.

Drake himself died eight years later on a raiding expedition in the Caribbean that went disastrously wrong. He was buried at sea, and great was the celebration when the news of his death reached Spain. In England, however, he became an instant hero, inspiring implausible tales of wizardry. According to one, he increased the size of his fleet by cutting a piece of wood into chips, each of which became — hey-presto! — a man-o'-war.

His legend has been revived particularly at times of national danger. In the early 1800s, when Napoleon's troops were poised to cross the Channel, an ancient drum was discovered which was said to have travelled everywhere with Drake, and the Victorian poet Sir Henry Newbolt imagined the old sea dog dying in the tropics on his final voyage, promising to heed the summons whenever England had need of him:

Take my drum to England, hang et by the shore,
Strike et when your powder's runnin' low;
If the Dons sight Devon, I'll quit the port o' Heaven,
An' drum them up the Channel as we drummed them long ago.

SIR JOHN'S JAKES

1592

TODAY WE ASSOCIATE SEWAGE DISPOSAL with water — the push of a button, the pull of a chain and whoosh . . . But conveniences were rarely so convenient in Tudor times. A few castles had 'houses of easement' situated over the waters of the moat, and Dick Whittington's famous 'Longhouse' (see p.13) had been built over the River Thames. One of the advantages of occupying the hundred or so homes built on the sixteenth-century London Bridge was the straight drop from privy to river — though this was also a hazard for passing boatmen.

For most people, a hole in the earth did the job — inside

a fenced enclosure or little hut at the back of the house. Moss or leaves served for toilet paper and a shovelful of earth for a flush. When the hole was full, you simply upped sticks and found, or made, a new hole.

At the other end of the social scale, Henry VIII had a private throne to suit his style and status. Decorated with ribbons, fringes and two thousand gold nails, his 'close stool' was a black velvet box concealing a pewter chamber pot whose regular clearing and cleaning was the job of the 'groom of the stool'.

His daughter Queen Elizabeth probably had a similar device, but in 1592 she was offered a novel alternative. While staying with her godson Sir John Harington at Kelston near Bath, she was invited to test his invention — the first modern water closet, complete with a seat and a lever by means of which you could flush water down from a cistern above. The Queen liked it so much she had one installed in her palace at Richmond.

Harington publicised his invention in a joke-filled book, *The Metamorphosis of Ajax*. The title itself was a pun — 'jakes' was the Elizabethan slang for lavatory — and the author supplied a helpful diagram for do-it-yourselfers showing how, for 30s 8d (around £250 today), you could build your own WC. It would make 'your worst privy as sweet as your best chamber', he promised — and his drawing showed that you could even keep your pet goldfish in the cistern.

Harington's WC was not the first. The Romans had flushing cisterns. But his design does seem to have been the original product of a lively mind. Elizabeth's multi-gifted godson amused her court with his translations of risqué foreign verses and, not surprisingly, bold wit that he was, he was never afraid to mention the unmentionable:

> *If leeks you leake, but do their smell disleeke, eat onions and*
> *   you shall not smell the leek.*
> *If you of onions would the scent expel,*
> *Eat garlic – that shall drown the onion smell.*
> *But against garlic's savour, if you smart,*
> *I know but one receipt. What's that? A fart.*

BY TIME SURPRISED

1603

B Y MARCH 1603 IT WAS CLEAR THAT ELIZABETH was dying. The faithful Doctor Dee had looked at the stars and advised her to move from Whitehall to her palace at airy Richmond. There she sat on the floor for days, propped up with embroidered cushions. With her finger in her mouth and her features, as ever, plastered with white, lead-based make-up, the sixty-nine-year-old monarch refused to eat, sleep or change her clothes.

'Madam, you must to bed,' urged Robert Cecil, who had become her chief minister following the death of his father William, Lord Burghley, in 1598.

'Little man! Little man!' retorted the Queen. 'Your father

would have known that "must" is not a word we use to princes.'

The closing years of her reign had not been happy ones. The great triumph of the Armada had been followed by still more warfare — with Spain, in Ireland, in France and in the Netherlands. War cost money, and three times more taxes had been levied in the fifteen years since 1588 than in the first thirty years of her reign. Harvests had been poor, prices high, trade depressed. Parliament complained bitterly at the growth of 'monopolies', the exclusive trading licences the Queen granted to favourites like Ralegh, who controlled the sales of tin and playing cards, and also the licensing of taverns. Steel, starch, salt, imported drinking glasses . . . the list of these privately controlled and taxed commodities was read out one day in Parliament. 'Is not bread there?' called out a sarcastic voice.

In 1601 discontented citizens had marched through the streets of London in support of the Earl of Essex, the arrogant young aristocrat who had dared to criticise and defy Elizabeth. She sent him to the block — a last flourish of the standard Tudor remedy for troublemakers — but that did not stop people laughing at her behind her back. Even her godson John Harington, the Jakes inventor, sniggered uncharitably at the out-of-touch monarch 'shut up in a chamber from her subjects and most of her servants . . . seldom seen but on holy days'. Sir Walter Ralegh put it more gallantly. The Queen, he said, was 'a lady whom time had surprised'.

Elizabeth had always refused to nominate an heir. She had no wish, she said, to contemplate her 'own winding sheet'. But by 1603 it was clear there could be only one successor — King James VI of Scotland, the son of Mary Queen of Scots. Now thirty-six, James had proved himself a canny ruler north of the border, and his bloodline was impeccable. He was the great-great-grandson of the first Tudor, Henry VII.

Robert Cecil had been corresponding secretly with James for months, and all through February and March the horses stood ready, staged at ten-mile intervals so that news of the Queen's death would reach Scotland without delay. On the evening of 23 March she fell unconscious and, waking only briefly, she died in the small hours of the 24th. As the messenger headed north, trumpeters, heralds, judges and barons were already processing through the streets of London to proclaim the new King James I.

Elizabeth I, Queen of Shakespeare, Ralegh, Drake and the Armada, had presided over one of the most glorious flowerings of English history and culture, and her success owed not a little to the adroitness with which she had avoided marriage. But this also meant that she was the last of her line. Her successor James Stuart and every subsequent English and British monarch has taken their descent not from Gloriana, but from Elizabeth's hated rival, Mary Queen of Scots.

5/11: ENGLAND'S
FIRST TERRORIST

1605

WITH HIS FLOWING MOUSTACHE AND LUXU-
rious beard, Guy Fawkes cut an elegant figure — he
looked like anything but a household servant as he lurked in
one of the cellars-to-rent below the Houses of Parliament
on the afternoon of 4 November 1605. He was wearing a
dark hat and cloak, and had strapped his spurs on to his riding boots, ready for a quick escape. But when the Lord
Chamberlain's guards came upon Guy in the candlelit cellar,
they believed his story. He was a domestic servant, he told
them — 'John Johnson' was the cover name he had prepared — and he had been checking on the piles of firewood

stacked against the wall. The search party went on their way, not thinking to rummage behind the dry kindling, where, if they had looked, they would have discovered thirty-six large barrels of gunpowder . . .

The notorious Gunpowder Plot was born of the injustice and disappointment that many English Catholics came to feel at the beginning of the reign of King James I. Their hopes had been high that the son of Mary Queen of Scots, their Catholic champion and martyr, would ease the legal persecution from which they suffered — and James duly had his mother's body dug up and reburied in Westminster Abbey. Mary lies there to this day, in a splendid tomb along-side Elizabeth — the two cousins, Catholic and Protestant, honoured equally in death.

But James knew he must live with the reality of a nation that defined itself as Protestant, and soon after his arrival in England he summoned a conference at Hampton Court to submit the Church of England to review by the growing number of evangelicals who wanted to weed out the 'impure' practices left over from Catholicism. As far as doctrine was concerned, the new King gave these 'Puritans' less than they wanted, but he did bow to their demands to enforce the anti-Catholic laws that Elizabeth had applied with a relatively light touch.

These laws were fierce. Anyone caught hearing the mass could be fined and sent to jail. Priests — many of whom survived in 'priest holes' hidden behind the panelling in the homes of rich Catholics — were liable to be punished by imprisonment or even death. Catholic children could not be baptised. The dying were denied the ceremony of extreme unction, their crucial step to heaven. Catholics could not study at university. If they failed to attend their local Anglican church they were classed as 'recusants' (we might say 'refuseniks'), and became liable to fines of £20 a month. The enforcement of recusancy fines was patchy, but £20 was a quite impossible penalty at a time when a yeoman, or 'middling', farmer was legally defined as someone whose land brought him forty shillings, or £2, per year.

'Catholics now saw their own country,' wrote Father William Weston, 'the country of their birth, turned into a ruthless and unloving land.'

State-sponsored oppression, frustration, hopelessness — from these bitter ingredients stemmed the extravagant scheme of Guy Fawkes and a dozen aggrieved young Catholics to blow up the King, his family, the Royal Council and all the members of the Protestant-dominated Houses of Parliament in one spectacular blast. Modern explosives experts have calculated that Guy's thirty-six barrels (5,500 pounds) of gunpowder would have caused 'severe structural damage' to an area within a radius of five hundred metres. Not only the Houses of Parliament, but Westminster Abbey and much of Whitehall would have been demolished in a terrorist gesture whose imaginative and destructive power stands comparison, for its time, with the planes that al-Qaeda's pilots crashed into New York's World Trade Center on 11 September 2001.

But as the Gunpowder Plotters' plan for scarcely imaginable slaughter became known in Catholic circles, someone felt they had to blow the whistle:

*My Lord, out of the love I bear to some of your friends, I have a
care of your preservation . . . [read an anonymous letter sent to a
Catholic peer, Lord Monteagle, on 26 October 1605] I would ad-
vise you, as you tender your life, to devise some excuse to shift of
your attendance at this Parliament . . . [and] retire yourself into
your country where you may expect the event in safety.*

Delivered at dusk by a tall stranger to a servant of Monteagle's outside his house in Hoxton on the north-east outskirts of London, this 'dark and doubtful letter' can be seen
today in the National Archives, and has inspired fevered debate among scholars: who betrayed the plot? The letter's au-
thorship has been attributed to almost every one of Guy
Fawkes's confederates — and even to Robert Cecil, Lord
Salisbury, James's chief minister, who organised the investi-
gation after Monteagle handed over the letter.

'John Johnson' fooled the first search party on the afternoon of 4 November, but not the second, who, lanterns in
hand, prodded their way through the cellars in the early
hours of the 5th, the very day Parliament was due to assem-
ble. Once arrested, he made no secret of his intention to
blow up King and lords. His only regret, he said, was that
his plan had not succeeded. It was 'the devil and not God'
who had betrayed the plot.

Torture soon extracted from Guy Fawkes that he was a
thirty-four-year-old Catholic from York who had fought in
the Netherlands on the Spanish side against the Dutch
Protestants. Like the letter that betrayed him, his successive
confessions can be read today: his signature starts off firm
and black, then degenerates to a tremulous and scarcely leg-

ible scratching as the rack does its dreadful work. Once Parliament had been destroyed, it turned out, the conspirators were planning to seize the King's nine-year-old daughter Princess Elizabeth, and install her as their puppet ruler.

Guy and his fellow-plotters suffered the ghastly penalties prescribed for traitors: they were hung, drawn and quartered. When Parliament reassembled, the first order of business was to institute 'a public thanksgiving to Almighty God every year on the fifth day of November' — the origin of our modern 'Bonfire Night'. But furious Protestants were not content with executions and prayers.

'This bloody stain and mark will never be washed out of Popish religion,' declared Sir Thomas Smith, one of the many who called for vengeance. Half a century after the fires of Smithfield, the Gunpowder Plot marked a further stage in the demonising of English Catholics, who, in the years that followed, were banned from practising law, serving in the army or navy as officers, or voting in elections. In 1614 one MP suggested Catholics be compelled to wear a yellow hat and shoes so they could be easily identified and 'hooted at' by true Englishmen.

This last proposal was, happily, judged to be unEnglish and went no further. But the Gunpowder Plot raises important moral issues to this day. Is violence permissible to a persecuted minority? And if you do strike back against a government that subjects you to state-sponsored terror — why are you the one called a terrorist?

KING JAMES'S
'AUTHENTICAL' BIBLE

1611

'NO MOR ENGLAND BOT GRATE BRITAINE,' noted a patriotic Scot in his diary, as James VI of Scotland and I of England rode out from Edinburgh to claim his southern kingdom in the spring of 1603. When the new King opened his first Parliament in London, he urged his English subjects to join more closely with Scotland — he called for a 'Union of Love' — and on 16 November he signed a decree creating a new Anglo-Scottish currency featuring a twenty-shilling piece called 'the Unite'. Sadly for James, his McPound proved impractical, but in 1604 he did initiate a project that would, over the years, make for unity in another sense, and in a context far wider than England and Scotland.

As the clerics debated at the Hampton Court conference in 1604 one of them suggested that there should be 'one only translation of the Bible to be authentical', and the King seized on the idea. 'One uniform translation' should be produced, he agreed, 'by the learned of both universities', to be reviewed by the 'chief learned of the church', then ratified by himself. 'Were I not a King,' he informed his bishops proudly, 'I would be a University man.'

Seven years, fifty-four translators and six committees later, the result of the King's initiative was the 'Authorised Version' that bears his name — the so-called King James Bible, 'Newly Translated out of the Originall tongues & with the former Translations diligently compared and revised by his Maiesties Speciall Comandement — Appointed to be read in Churches'.

For two hundred and fifty years the King James Bible would set the standard for phraseology, rhythm and syntax wherever in the world English speakers gathered — an English grammar and literature lesson in its own right. Sunday after Sunday its sonorous cadences filtered into the English consciousness, shaping thought patterns as well as language — and this was just as King James's scholarly committees intended: the surviving records of their deliberations make clear that they searched constantly for the words that would not only read better but *sound* better, for this was a lectern Bible, designed above all to be read out and listened to.

The dream of William Tyndale — and before that of John Wycliffe — had finally come true. Here was a Bible that could be understood by every ploughboy, built on a spare and simple vocabulary of only eight thousand different words — and time after time the reviewing committees decided that William Tyndale's translations were the best. They made only small changes to his original phrases, so that, in the end, eighty per cent of this royally 'authorised' version came from the man who had been tracked down by Henry VIII's agents seventy-five years earlier and had been burned at the stake.

'Our Father, which art in heaven, hallowed be thy name . . .' Even today, in our relatively non-religious age, these memorable Tyndale-King James lines may well be the most frequently repeated set of sentences in the English language.

'SPOILT CHILD' AND THE
PILGRIM FATHERS

1616

IN THE SPRING OF 1616 THE TOAST OF LONDON
was an exotic young arrival from the New World —
'Pocahontas', the beautiful twenty-one-year-old daughter of
Powhatan, chief of the Algonquins of coastal Virginia. Her
tribal name had been Matoaka, but her family had nicknamed her the 'naughty one', or 'spoilt child' — and it was
under her nickname that she had been brought to London
to celebrate the nine-year survival of Jamestown, Virginia.
This was England's first permanent colony in North America, established in Chesapeake Bay, a hundred miles or so
north of Ralegh's 'lost colony' of Roanoke.

Wined and dined and taken to London's flourishing

theatres, Pocahontas was presented to King James I, after whom the new settlement had been named. Her visit spearheaded a publicity drive by the investors of the Virginia Company who were looking for new colonists and partners. Much was made of the young woman's conversion to Christianity and her marriage to a wealthy tobacco planter, John Rolfe, by whom she had a son. Even before Pocahontas died of pneumonia (or possibly tuberculosis) in March 1617, to be buried at Gravesend in Kent, the Indian 'princess' had come to symbolise the prospect of good relations between the new colonists and the native population.

That hope, we now know, was a cruel illusion. The modern United States of America has been built upon the systematic destruction and dispossession of its native population — and the few reliable facts we possess about the life of Pocahontas place a question mark over her myth. In 1612 she had been captured and held to ransom in the course of a savage series of attacks and reprisals between colonists and locals, and according to the Powhatan nation of American Indians who champion her cause today, the marriage of Pocahontas to the older, wealthy widower John Rolfe was anything but a love match: it was the price of her release.

The Never-Never Land aspects of transatlantic exploration were made clear the following year when Sir Walter Ralegh, now sixty-seven and a creaking relic of the glory days of Elizabeth, sailed into Plymouth after a failed attempt to locate El Dorado, the fabled city of gold that was said to lie in the rainforests of South America. Having flirted with ill-judged notions of conspiracy in the early months of James's reign, Ralegh had spent a dozen years imprisoned in the Tower before winning temporary release on his far-fetched promise to bring back the treasures of El Dorado. But he failed to locate the city. Furthermore, his frustrated followers attacked a Spanish settlement, and it suited James to sacrifice the old Elizabethan to the Spanish protests that followed. "'Tis a sharp remedy,' Ralegh remarked as he felt the edge of the axe in New Palace Yard on 29 October 1618, 'but a sure one for all ills.'

The flamboyant champion of England's empire overseas went to his death not long before his dream — or something like it — became reality. In September 1620 the Pilgrim Fathers set sail from Plymouth in their merchant ship, the *Mayflower*. They came mainly from the village of Scrooby in Nottinghamshire, where they had pursued a category of Puritanism known as 'Separatism'. Abandoning the hope that they could 'purify' the Church of England of its papist taints, the Scrooby Separatists looked abroad, and in 1608 had exiled themselves to Protestant Holland. Among their leaders were the local postmaster William Brewster, and a fervent Yorkshireman, William Bradford, who would later write the story of their great adventure.

But Bradford, Brewster and their companions did not find the welcome they expected in Holland. While they were allowed to practise their religion, Dutch guild regulations prevented them from practising their trades. So they were after economic as well as religious freedom when they boarded the *Mayflower* in the summer of 1620, landing on Cape Cod, in modern Massachusetts, on 9 November. To govern themselves they drew up the 'Mayflower Compact', the first written constitution in the Americas — indeed, the first written constitution in the English language, in which the authority of government was explicitly based on the consent of the governed. And having sailed from Plymouth, they named their colony Plymouth.

In the next two decades Plymouth Colony inspired more than twenty thousand settlers to create new lives for themselves in the stockaded villages of 'New England' — and it also inspired the great American festival of Thanksgiving. Tradition dates this back to November 1621 when, after half Plymouth's pilgrims had died of disease and famine, the local Indians came to their rescue with a feast of turkey, corn on the cob, sweet potatoes and cranberries.

The rescue of 1621 is well documented, but more than two centuries were to elapse before we find Thanksgiving being celebrated routinely on an annual basis. Not until 1863 was Abraham Lincoln encouraged by the rediscovery of William Bradford's history *Of Plymouth Plantation* to reinvent the tradition and declare Thanksgiving a national holiday.

We should also, perhaps, revise our image of the Pilgrim Fathers all wearing sober black costumes with white collars and big buckles on their shoes. Shoe buckles did not come into fashion until the late 1660s, and, as for the colonists' costumes, as inventoried on their deaths by the Plymouth plantation court, they sound more like those of pixies than pilgrims: *Mayflower* passenger John Howland died with two red waistcoats in his travelling chest; William Bradford also owned a red waistcoat, along with a green gown and a suit with silver buttons, while the wardrobe of William Brewster, the former postmaster of Scrooby, featured green breeches, a red cap and a fine 'violet' coat.

THE ARK OF THE
JOHN TRADESCANTS

1622

Ananas comosus

THE JOHN TRADESCANTS, FATHER AND SON, were England's first master gardeners. John Sr made his name in the final years of Elizabeth's reign, and was then hired in 1609 by Robert Cecil, 1st Lord Salisbury, to beautify the gardens of his grand new home, Hatfield House in Hertfordshire. John travelled to Holland to purchase the newly fashionable flower, the tulip, and spent no less than eighty shillings of Cecil's money (the equivalent of £440 today) on sacks of bulbs. In search of more exotic plants, he joined a trading expedition to Russia in 1618, and two years later accompanied a squadron of English warships sent to

North Africa to quell the Barbary pirates. Among the specimens he brought home was the hardy perennial beloved of modern gardeners, tradescantia.

But John was interested in more than plants. He started collecting local artefacts and curiosities on his travels, and this passion of his received a powerful boost in 1622 when he became gardener to George Villiers, Duke of Buckingham, the controversial favourite of King James I. Buckingham was Lord Admiral, and it was not long before the navy was instructing all English merchants engaged in trade with the New World to be on the lookout for a lengthy list of rarities — in fact 'any thing that is strange' — drawn up by John Tradescant.

By the 1630s, the Tradescant collection filled several rooms of the family house at Lambeth, just across the Thames from Westminster, and John decided to open his 'rarities' to the public. Taking biblical inspiration, he called England's first ever museum 'The Ark'. The public flocked to gaze at such novelties as the hat and lantern taken from Guy Fawkes when he was arrested under the Houses of Parliament, alongside over a thousand named varieties of plants, flowers and trees — an apparently odd but enduring combination of English enthusiasms that lives on in the popularity of such TV programmes as *Gardeners' World* and *Antiques Roadshow*.

After John's death in 1638, his son took over the collection, proving an even more adventurous traveller than his father. He crossed the Atlantic three times to bring back the pineapple, the yucca and the scarlet runner bean, along with the Virginia creeper whose green leaves go flame-red in autumn. In his later years John Jr joined forces with Elias Ashmole, an ambitious lawyer who had helped catalogue the collection, but after John's death Ashmole became embroiled in a series of disputes with Tradescant's widow Hester.

One morning, in April 1678, Hester Tradescant was found dead, apparently drowned in the garden pool at her Lambeth home. Foul play was ruled out, but Ashmole took control of Tradescant's Ark. The collection came to form the nucleus of the Ashmolean Museum at Oxford — where you can still see Guy Fawkes's hat and lantern.

GOD'S LIEUTENANT IN EARTH

1629

WHEN JAMES I'S SECOND-BORN SON PRINCE
Charles arrived in London at the beginning of his
father's reign, courtiers hesitated to join his retinue. The
child was sickly and backward — he could easily die and his
household vanish, leaving them high and dry. By his fourth
birthday in November 1604 the young prince was still not
walking properly, and his father was so worried by his slow
speech and stutter that he 'was desirous that the string under his tongue should be cut'.

But Charles was not a quitter. The plodding prince worked
hard at overcoming his disabilities, particularly after 1612
when his more obviously gifted elder brother Henry died of

typhoid. By the time Charles I succeeded his father in March 1625, he was a young man of some grit, principle and piety, already displaying the taste that would make him, arguably, England's greatest royal patron of the arts. But the admirable determination he had shown in his childhood now verged on obstinacy, which was fed by the big idea that would eventually bring disaster on his family — the Divine Right of Kings.

The notion had been planted by his writerly father, James, who quoted lengthy passages from the Bible in his pamphlet *The Trew Law of Free Monarchies* in support of his argument that an anointed monarch was 'God's Lieutenant in earth'. This view was taken for granted by the absolute monarchs of early modern Europe, but the self-righteous James had turned it into a lecture directed at his 'honest and obedient subjects'. A people could no more depose their King, he told them, than sons could replace their father. 'I have at length prooved,' he concluded, 'that the King is above the law.'

When it came to practical politics, James himself had never pushed his ideas to the limit, particularly when, south of the border, he found himself dealing with the touchy squires and merchants who dominated England's House of Commons. But Charles lacked his father's subtlety. He felt personally affronted when on his accession Parliament declined to vote him the usual supply of customs revenues for life, granting the money for one year only. Puritan MPs were suspicious of Charles's French Catholic wife and of his personal preference for church ceremonial — and no one liked his reliance on the Duke of Buckingham, the unpopular favourite he had taken over from his father. 'In the government,' complained one member, 'there wanteth good advice.' But rather than negotiate in the style of his father — or cajole, as the imperious Queen Elizabeth would have done — Charles lost his temper. He dissolved Parliament in August 1625 and the following year started raising funds with 'forced loans', the ancient, discredited tactic of Empson and Dudley (see p. 81) which Charles now extended from a handful of rich targets to most of the tax-paying community. When his Chief Justice, Sir Randolph Crew, questioned the legality of this non-parliamentary levy, Charles dismissed him; more than seventy non-payers were sent to prison.

These were serious issues to the MPs whose predecessors had made the laws that had helped Henry VIII break with Rome. James had written about kings being above the law — Charles was trying to put theory into practice. When a shortage of funds compelled him to summon Parliament again in 1628, an angry House of Commons wasted no time in preparing a statement of fundamental principles, the Petition of Right, which prohibited non-parliamentary taxation and arbitrary imprisonment. After some prevarication, Charles signed the petition, but he did so with ill grace — and then, that August, his friend and confidant Buckingham was assassinated in Portsmouth.

The murder was the work of a deranged Puritan, John Felton, who had been incited by parliamentary denunciations of Buckingham as 'the grievance of all grievances', and Charles blamed his critics in Parliament for the killing. He felt bitterly wounded by the explosion of popular joy that greeted the news of Buckingham's death, and it turned his deepening dislike of Parliament into a grudge match that came to a head in the spring of 1629.

The issue was religion. Sir John Eliot, the eloquent Puritan MP who had led the assaults on both Buckingham and forced loans, had produced a resolution against what were known as 'Arminian' church practices, so-called after the Dutch theologian Jacob Arminius whose English admirers had called for a return to church ceremonial. This cause was championed by Charles's recently appointed Bishop of London, William Laud, who was busy restoring neglected rituals to the Church of England. In what we would describe as a battle between High and Low Church, Charles sided enthusiastically with ritual, and rightly interpreted the Puritan attack on Arminianism as a snub to his royal authority. He sent orders to Westminster to halt all discussion immediately.

The Commons responded with a defiance that would become historic. Heedless of the King's words, the debate continued. One MP, Sir Miles Hobart, locked the door against the indignant hammerings of the King's messenger, while the burly MP for Dorchester, Denzil Holles, forcibly held down the Speaker, Sir John Finch, in his chair. The Speaker was the Commons' servant, not the King's, Finch was told, and Sir John Eliot took the floor to denounce 'innovations in religion' and royal interference with Parliament's right to speak. 'None had gone about to break parliaments,' he declared, 'but in the end parliaments had broken them.'

Cries of 'Aye, Aye, Aye' rang out around the chamber, and Eliot's resolution against 'Popery or Arminianism' was duly acclaimed, along with a further condemnation of taxation without parliamentary assent. Anyone who disagreed or disobeyed — and this presumably included the King — 'shall be reputed a capital enemy to this kingdom and commonwealth . . . He shall likewise be reputed a betrayer of the liberties of England.'

But two days later, Hobart, Holles, Eliot and six other leaders of the protest were on their way to the Tower. Charles had the dissidents arrested, then dissolved Parliament on 10 March. God's Lieutenant had decided he could rule England more smoothly without it.

'ALL MY BIRDS HAVE FLOWN'

1642

CHARLES I ATTEMPTED TO RULE ENGLAND without Parliament for eleven years, from 1629 to 1640, and he started off well enough. He made peace with Spain and France and, alongside his French wife Henrietta Maria, presided over a well-ordered court where art, music and drama flourished. Under his auspices, the Church of England was stringently administered by William Laud who, as Archbishop of Canterbury after 1633, organised diocesan inspections that tested the conformity of every priest and parish. Laud's efficient policy style came to be known as 'Thorough', and it was matched by Sir Thomas Wentworth, a former Member of Parliament who administered first the north and then Ireland for Charles, before rising to become his principal minister, ennobled as the Earl of Strafford.

Back in 1628, as MP for Yorkshire, Wentworth had spoken out in favour of the Petition of Right, yet he came to feel that many of his fellow-parliamentarians went too far in their attacks on King and Crown — a view that was shared by many. The austere and driven Puritans whose voices rang out loudest in the Commons were even calling for the removal of bishops from the Church of England. Such extremism fortified moderate support for the King, and it was Charles's tragedy that he would waste England's deep-rooted conservatism and loyalty to the Crown. As his own man Laud later put it, Charles I was 'a gracious prince who neither knew how to be, nor to be made, great'.

One of the virtues of raising money through Parliament was that it minimised direct conflict between taxpayer and King. But as Charles exploited ancient and obscure sources of revenue like the duty of seaport towns to supply the King with ships, solid citizens came into head-to-head conflict with the Crown. To widespread support, the opposition to 'ship money' was led by a prosperous Buckinghamshire landowner, John Hampden, who fought the tax in court, effectively contending that it was the King who was the lawbreaker here.

As so often, religion provoked even deeper issues of due process and fair play. When in 1634 the Puritan lawyer William Prynne denounced as immoral the court masques in which the King and his wife liked to dance, Charles's arbitrary Court of Star Chamber (evolved from the Royal Council of earlier times) ordered that his ears be cut off.

Three years later the incorrigible Prynne turned his holy criticism on the bishops — only to have what survived of his ears sliced away.

Hampden and Prynne became national heroes thanks to the printed newsletters — early versions of newspapers — that were beginning to circulate between London and the provinces. These publicised the political and religious issues at stake, usually favouring the underdog, while primitive woodcuts provided dramatic images that got the message to the two-thirds of the population who could not read. One cartoon showed a smiling Archbishop Laud dining off a dish of Prynne's severed ears.

Feelings were running high in 1640 when Charles reluctantly resumed dealing with Parliament. His attempt to take 'Thorough' to Scotland and to impose the English Prayer Book (against Laud's better judgement) on Scotland's Presbyterians had led to the so-called Bishops' Wars that drained the royal treasury dry. The early months of 1640 had seen an army of rebellious Scots occupying the north of England, and the King was urgently in need of money. But his parliamentary critics were bitterly determined that he should pay a price for it.

Strafford and Laud were their first targets, both indicted for treason as Charles's accomplices in what would later be known as the 'Eleven Years Tyranny'. Strafford was sent to trial in March 1641, charged with being the 'principal author and promoter of all those counsels which had exposed the kingdom to so much ruin'. When he defended himself so ably in court that an acquittal seemed possible, the Commons contrived another way to get him. They quickly passed a bill of attainder, a blunt instrument that baldly declared Strafford's guilt without need of legal process, and as Charles hesitated to sign the attainder, mobs of shaven-headed apprentices roamed the London streets baying for the blood of 'Black Tom the Tyrant'.

The campaign against Thomas Strafford was directed by John Pym, the veteran MP for Calne in Wiltshire who, a dozen years earlier, had been Sir John Eliot's principal lieutenant in the battle for the Petition of Right. Now Pym masterminded the entire parliamentary assault on royal powers, plotting with the Scottish rebels to maintain pressure on the King while also stirring up the London mobs. On 10 May 1641, fearing for the safety of his wife and children, Charles signed Strafford's attainder, and two days later his faithful servant went to the block in front of a jubilant crowd over one hundred thousand strong.

Having secured one victim, Parliament's radicals turned to the practical business of ensuring that personal rule could never be revived. In February that year the Triennial Act had held that Parliament, if not summoned by the King, must automatically reassemble after three years. Now followed an act against dissolving Parliament without its consent, another to abolish ship money, and acts to shut down the Court of Star Chamber, which had sliced off Prynne's ears, along with the Court of High Commission through which Laud had exercised his control over the Church.

On 1 December came the climax — a 'Grand Remonstrance on the State of the Kingdom', which set out no less than 204 complaints against Charles and his eleven years of personal rule. As the Commons went through their list of grievances, the debates escalated into a raucous public event to match the dragging-down of Strafford, with delegations riding in from Essex, Kent and Sussex to shout their protests outside Parliament. Many moderates became alarmed. They rallied to the royal cause and Pym's Remonstrance only just scraped through the Commons, by 159 votes to 148.

One hundred and forty-eight worried MPs was a workable base on which Charles I might have moved towards compromise — and there was every possibility that the Lords would reject the Remonstrance. But God's Lieutenant did not do compromise, and his hurt pride would not let him delay. Bitterly remorseful and blaming himself for Strafford's fate, on Monday 3 January 1642 Charles instructed his Attorney General to commence treason proceedings against his five bitterest critics in the Commons: John Pym, John Hampden, Denzil Holles, Arthur Hazelrig and William Strode, along with Viscount Mandeville, a leading reformer in the House of Lords.

Next day Charles marched to the Parliament House in Westminster with a party of guards, intending to lay hands on the culprits himself — an extraordinarily risky and melodramatic gesture into which he was tempted by Pym and his four companions, who had set themselves up as bait. Having advertised their presence in the Commons that morning, the five Members then monitored the King's progress down Whitehall.

When Charles entered the Commons chamber, he requested the Speaker, William Lenthall, to yield him his seat and to point out Pym and the others. Falling to his knees, Lenthall replied that it was not for him to either see or speak but as the House desired. There was no precedent for this situation. No King of England had ever interrupted a session of the House of Commons. "'Tis no matter,' declared Charles, 'I think my eyes are as good as another's', and he cast his eyes along the benches as the MPs stood bareheaded and in silence. Through the open door they could see the royal guards, some of whom were cocking their pistols, playfully pretending to mark down their men — until melodrama turned to anticlimax.

'All my birds have flown,' admitted Charles, disconsolately conceding defeat. Having set their trap, the five had made good their escape, slipping down to the river, where a boat took them into hiding in the City. As the crestfallen King turned on his heel to leave the chamber, the suddenly emboldened Members reminded him of their rights and let out catcalls of 'Privilege! Privilege!' at his retreating and humiliated back.

The debacle marked a breaking point. Compromise was no longer possible between an obstinate monarch and a defiant Parliament, and six days later, on 10 January 1642, Charles slipped out of Whitehall with his family. He stopped briefly at Hampton Court. Then Henrietta Maria headed for Holland with the crown jewels, hoping to raise money, while Charles rode towards York, intent on raising the army he would need to fight the Civil War.

ROUNDHEADS V. CAVALIERS

1642-8

LADY MARY BANKES WAS A FORMIDABLE woman, the mother of fourteen children. When the Civil War broke out in August 1642 it fell to her to defend the family home at Corfe Castle in Dorset. Her husband was a senior judge and a privy councillor, so when the King had gone north to raise his standard that summer Sir John Bankes followed. He soon found himself, like all the King's councillors, denounced by Parliament as a traitor.

Down in Dorset, the local parliamentary commander anticipated little trouble when he arrived at Corfe to take the surrender of the Bankes's home. But he had not reckoned on the valiant Lady Mary, who shut the gates against him. When his men attempted to scale the walls they found themselves showered with rocks and burning embers thrown by the family's loyal retainers — cooks and chambermaids included. Even a prize of £20 (£2,240 today) offered to the first man to reach the battlements attracted no takers. Hearing of royalist troops in the nearby town of Dorchester, the parliamentarians slunk away.

It took an act of treachery to capture Corfe three years later. One February night in 1646, an accomplice in the garrison opened the gates to fifty parliamentary troops disguised as royalists, and Lady Bankes, a widow since her husband's death at Oxford two years previously, was arrested. Parliament confiscated their lands and decided to 'slight' Corfe Castle: they stacked the main towers with gunpowder barrels, then exploded them.

The bravery of Lady Mary and the spectacular ruins of her castle that loom over Corfe to this day illustrate the drama of England's Civil War and the damage it wreaked. Modern estimates suggest that one in every four or five adult males was caught up in the fighting: 150 towns suffered serious destruction; 11,000 houses were burned or demolished and 55,000 people made homeless — these were the years when the German word *plündern,* to plunder, came into the language, brought over by Charles's loot-happy cavalry commander, his nephew Prince Rupert of the Rhine. Nearly 4 per cent of England's population died in the fighting or from war-related disease — a higher proportion, even, than died in World War I. 'Whose blood stains the walls of our towns and defiles our land?' lamented Bulstrode Whitelock to the House of Commons in 1643. 'Is it not all English?'

The Civil War was not like the Wars of the Roses, when everyday life had largely carried on as normal. The clash between King and Parliament involved the most fundamental question — how should the country be ruled? And to this was added the profound differences in religion that bitterly divided families and split friend from friend. Sir William Waller and Sir Ralph Hopton had been comrades-in-arms in the early 1620s, fighting Catholics on the continent. But now they found themselves on opposing sides, Sir William supporting Parliament because of his Puritan beliefs, Sir Ralph feeling that he must stay loyal to his monarch. 'That great God which is the searcher of my heart knows with what a sad sense I go upon this service,' wrote Waller in distress to his old friend in 1643, 'and with what a perfect hatred I detest this war without an enemy . . . [But] we are both upon the stage and must act those parts that are assigned us in this tragedy.'

Both 'Roundhead' and 'Cavalier' were originally terms of abuse. Before the war began, royalists derided the 'round heads' of the crop-haired London apprentices who had rioted outside Parliament in late December 1641 calling for the exclusion of bishops and Catholic peers from the House of Lords. In retaliation the parliamentarians dubbed their opponents *caballeros*, after the Spanish troopers notorious for their brutality against the Dutch Protestants. When Charles I heard this rendered into English as 'cavalier' he decided that he liked the associations of nobility and horsemanship, and encouraged his followers to adopt the word.

In October 1642 came the first great battle of the Civil War, at Edgehill, north of the royal headquarters at Oxford.

Outcome: indecisive. In the year that followed, the balance swung the King's way. But in July 1644 the two sides met en masse at Marston Moor, outside York, and Parliament was triumphant.

'God made them as stubble to our swords,' boasted the plain-spoken commander of the parliamentary cavalry, Oliver Cromwell. In a famous letter to his fellow-officers from East Anglia, this stocky gentleman farmer who was fast becoming the inspiration of the parliamentary cause described what he looked for in his soldiers: 'I had rather have a plain russet-coated captain what knows what he fights for, and loves what he knows,' he wrote, 'than that which you call a gentleman and is nothing else.' When it came to recruiting, explained the Puritan preacher Richard Baxter, 'none would be such engaged fighting men as the religious'.

Religion was the inspiration of the New Model Army, the 22,000-strong professional fighting force that Cromwell and the parliamentary commander Sir Thomas Fairfax were now organising to replace the system of regional militias. Its regiments sang hymns, refrained from drinking, and made a point of listening to sermons. Royalists nicknamed this new army the 'Noddle' in mockery of its constant godly head-bobbing in prayer, but sober discipline and holy certainty brought results. On 14 June 1645 at Naseby, just south of Leicester, the red-tunicked Noddle won the decisive victory of the Civil War, taking some five thousand prisoners, securing £100,000 in jewels and booty, and — worst of all from Charles's point of view — capturing the King's private correspondence. Soon published in pamphlet form, *The King's Cabinet Opened* revealed that Charles had been plotting to hire foreign mercenaries and to repeal the laws against Roman Catholics.

For Oliver Cromwell and the Puritan members of the New Model Army, this was the ultimate betrayal. It was proof that the King could never be trusted. Righteous voices were raised demanding the ultimate accounting with 'Charles Stuart, that man of blood'.

The Battle of Naseby left Charles I at the mercy of an army as convinced of their divine right as he was.

BEHOLD THE HEAD
OF A TRAITOR!

1649

EARLY IN JUNE 1647 CORNET GEORGE JOYCE led five hundred horsemen of the New Model Army to Holmby House in Northamptonshire. In civilian life, Joyce was a tailor. Now he was a cornet of horse, an officer who carried the flag — and his orders were to capture the King.

The Battle of Naseby had finished the Cavaliers as a fighting force, and having vainly tried to play off his English and Scottish enemies against each other, Charles had ended up in parliamentary custody at Holmby. But Parliament and the army had fallen out over what should be done with their tricky royal prisoner, and now the army took the initiative. They would seize Charles for themselves. At dawn on 3 June, the King walked through the gates of Holmby to find Cornet Joyce waiting for him, with his fully armed fighting men lined up at attention.

'I pray you, Mr Joyce . . .' asked the King, 'tell me what commission you have?'

'Here is my commission,' replied the cornet of horse.

'Where?' asked the King.

'Behind,' replied Joyce, pointing to his ranks of red-coated troopers.

The dramatic break between army and Parliament had occurred four months earlier, in February 1647, when MPs had voted to disband the New Model Army and to send its members home. England was exhausted by war, and reflecting the national mood, Parliament's leaders set about negotiating a settlement with the King.

But the men who had risked their lives and seen their companions fall in battle were incensed. Parliament was not only dismissing them with pay owing, it was negotiating with the Antichrist, planning to restore Charles — along with his popish wife and advisers — to the throne. 'We were not a mere mercenary army,' complained 'The Declaration of the Army' of June that year, 'hired to serve any arbitrary power of the state, but [were] called forth . . . to the defence of the people's just right and liberties.'

Radical ideas had flourished in the war years. Once the army had taken custody of the King it had the power to shape the way England would be governed, and in October 1647 the Council of the Army met at St Mary's Church in the village of Putney, south-west of London, to discuss future action. The agenda was set by the utopian ideas of the

'Levellers', who were demanding that Parliament be elected by all men, not just on the existing franchise of property-holders and tradesmen. The Levellers wanted no less than to get rid of the lords and the monarchy. 'The poorest he that is in England has a life to live as the greatest he,' declared Colonel Thomas Rainsborough, as he kicked off discussion in what became known as 'the Putney Debates'.

The case for the 'grandees' — the established property-holders and others who held a 'fixed interest in the kingdom' — was put by Cromwell's son-in-law Henry Ireton. But the army's groundbreaking discussions were cut short. Ensconced upriver at Hampton Court, Charles took fright at the reports reaching him from Putney, and on 11 November he escaped under cover of darkness, riding south towards the Channel.

There is no telling what might have happened if, having reached the coast, Charles had then taken ship for France. But, not for the first time, the King turned in the wrong direction, heading for the Isle of Wight, where he had been informed — incorrectly — that the governor had royalist sympathies. In no time Charles found himself behind bars, in Carisbrook Castle, his abortive escape bid the prelude to what became known as the Second Civil War. Royalists now rose in revolt in Kent, Essex, Yorkshire and Wales, to be followed by an invasion by a Scottish army, lured south on a secret promise from Charles that he would introduce Presbyterianism to England and suppress the wilder Puritan sects.

It was the last straw. Parliament and the New Model Army were reunited in their fury at Charles's enduring intransigence, and these risings of the Second Civil War were put down with unforgiving savagery. When the King's chaplain, Michael Hudson, was cornered on the roof at Woodcroft Hall in Lincolnshire, parliamentary troopers refused his appeal for mercy, flinging him and his companions into the moat below. As Hudson clung on to a drainage spout, his fingers were slashed off, and he was retrieved from the moat only to have his tongue cut out before being executed.

The King was treated no less ruthlessly. Cromwell and the generals were now resolved to bring him to trial, and realising that a majority of MPs still favoured some sort of compromise, they organised a *coup d'état*. Early on the morning of 6 December 1648, a detachment of horsemen and foot-soldiers under Colonel Thomas Pride surrounded both Houses of Parliament and arrested or turned away all suspected compromisers and royalist sympathisers — more than 140 members.

'Pride's purge' made possible the final act of the drama. On New Year's Day 1649, the hard-core of MPs remaining voted 'to erect a high Court of Justice to try King Charles for treason', and on 20 January the trial began. The only judge who would risk the terrible responsibility of presiding over the court was an obscure provincial justice, John Bradshaw. But even he, despite being a committed republican, was so fearful that he wore armour beneath his robes and had had his beaver hat lined with steel. The King, for his part, contemptuously declined to remove his own hat as he took his seat beneath the hammer-beam roof of Westminster Hall. This contrived court, he maintained doggedly during one hearing after another, had no right to try him: he, more than his judges, stood for the liberties of the people. 'If power without law may make laws . . .' he declared, 'I do not know what subject he is in England that can be sure of his life.'

It was to no avail. Witnesses were summoned to testify they had seen the King rallying his troops at Edgehill, Naseby and on other battlefields, thus proving him guilty of waging war on Parliament and people. He was thus found guilty as a 'Tyrant, Traitor, Murderer, and Public Enemy to the good people of this Nation'. Death 'by severing the head from his body' was to be his fate.

Ten days later, on 30 January, Charles walked out on to the raised scaffold outside his splendid Banqueting House that stands to this day, just across Whitehall from Downing Street. It was a piercingly cold afternoon. The Thames had frozen, and the King had put on an extra shirt so he should not be seen to shiver.

'A subject and a sovereign are clean different things,' he declared defiantly in a long oration in which he denounced the arbitrary power of the sword that had made him 'the Martyr of the People'. Then, more prosaically, he asked the executioner, 'Does my hair trouble you?' — tucking his straggling grey locks into a nightcap to leave his neck bare.

The axe fell, severing the King's head with a single blow, and the executioner leaned down to pick it up with the standard cry — 'Behold the head of a traitor!' But the crowd, estimated at several thousand, scarcely cheered. Instead, recalled one seventeen-year-old boy later, the cry was greeted with 'such a groan as I have never heard before and desire I may never hear again'.

'TAKE AWAY THIS BAUBLE!'

1653

THE EXECUTION OF CHARLES I WAS THE SINGLE
most remarkable event in the course of English history —
and the person who brought it to pass has a claim to being
England's most remarkable man. Until almost the last moment, Oliver Cromwell had shared the fears many felt at the
enormity of cutting off the King's head. But when the death
warrant was finally presented for signature to the apprehen-
sive judges, it was Cromwell who bullied the requisite number into signing. He shouted down the waverers, flicked ink
at them, and, in one case, actually held down a doubter's
hand to the page until he signed.

In a portrait by the painter Samuel Cooper we can study

the features of the fifty-year-old Cromwell at the moment he became the most powerful living Englishman. His nose is bulbous, his eyes large and strikingly blue; a dusting of salt-and-pepper whiskers conceals a mole beneath his lower lip and there is another, the size of a pea, dark and shiny, above his right brow. 'The mirror does not flatter me,' he told the painter. 'Nor should you, Mr Cooper. I'll have it warts and all.'

Cromwell was a curious mixture of arrogance and humility, ruthlessly sweeping aside obstacles, while also prey to depression in the opinion of some modern historians — he was once treated for 'melancholy' by the exiled Huguenot physician Turquet de Mayerne. In addition, he suffered from bronchitis, though his wheeziness didn't inhibit the 'eloquence full of fervour' with which he came to the attention of the House of Commons; the MP for Huntingdon was sometimes seen with a piece of red flannel wrapped comfortingly around his throat.

His certainty of the rightness of his cause came from a deep and austere Puritan faith that set him on an inescapable collision course with the High Church policies of Charles I. At one stage Cromwell contemplated joining the thousands of Separatists who were seeking their religious freedom in the Americas. Instead he stayed, rising meteorically through the ranks of the parliamentary armies to find himself charged with the task of creating a New World at home.

Following Charles I's execution, a series of votes in the purged House of Commons abolished the House of Lords and the monarchy, and on 16 May 1649 England was declared a 'Commonwealth', ruled through Parliament by a Council of State of which Cromwell was a member. He was appointed Lieutenant General of the Commonwealth's armies, and in 1649-50 commanded ruthless campaigns against revolts in Ireland — where he massacred Catholics with a brutality that stirs resentful memories to this day — and also in Scotland, which had briefly dared to crown Charles's twenty-year-old son as Charles II. These successes capped a military career that gave Cromwell a victory tally of won 30, lost 0. As he returned triumphantly from each campaign, he was fêted like Caesar.

Like Caesar, too, he was drawn irresistibly towards political power. 'Take away this bauble!' he angrily declared in April 1653, as he strode into the House of Commons with a company of musketeers and pointed at the symbol of parliamentary authority, the ceremonial golden staff, or mace, which was set on the table in front of the Speaker.

Since 1648, when Colonel Thomas Pride had excluded those MPs likely to oppose putting Charles I on trial, the House of Commons had been a wildly unrepresentative body. Derided as the 'Rump', or remnant, its little clique of surviving members — just 140 or so — had only paid lip service to the problem, solemnly debating the surrender of their power for more than four years, while greedily hanging on to its perks and profits. 'You are no parliament, I say you are no parliament,' declaimed the exasperated Cromwell. 'I will put an end to your sitting.'

His alternative fared no better. The Nominated, or 'Barebones', Parliament (so nicknamed after the MP for London, the leather-seller turned preacher, Praise-God Barbon) was an assembly of Puritan worthies selected by local churches on such criteria as how many times the candidates prayed each day. First meeting in July 1653, this 'Parliament of Saints' dissolved itself after only five months, pushing Cromwell ever closer towards the option by which he had been tempted, but had been resisting, for so long.

King Oliver I? Cromwell's critics had long accused him of desiring nothing less; and his supporters urged him to take the crown. A royal House of Cromwell was not an impossible concept in a society that found it difficult to imagine life without a king. But Cromwell's conscience would not let him. It would have betrayed everything he stood for — and the idea was, in any case, totally unacceptable to the army. In December 1653 he was proclaimed Lord Protector of England, and when he accepted this new dignity he was careful to dress in a plain black outfit with grey worsted stockings to emphasise that this was not a coronation.

The new Lord Protector believed that government should be 'for the people's good, not what pleases them', and for nearly five years he force-fed England a diet of godliness. Since the start of the Civil War, Parliament's Puritans had been legislating for virtue, and now Cromwell put this into practice — particularly after July 1655 when he set up a network of military governors, the 'major generals'. Sunday sports were quite literally spoiled: horseracing, cockfighting, bear-baiting, bowling, shooting, dancing, wrestling — all were banned on the Sabbath. It was an offence on any day to dance around a maypole or to be caught swearing: children under twelve who uttered profanities could be whipped. Fornicators were sent to prison, and for the only time in English history (apart from the reign of King Canute), adultery was punishable by death.

Human nature won through, of course. In many localities these Puritan regulations were scarcely enforced. But they have rather unfairly defined Cromwell's place in history. He never became King Oliver, but he *was* crowned King Kill-Joy — and when he died of malaria in September 1658 there was dancing in the streets. It was 'the joyfullest funeral that ever I saw', wrote John Evelyn, 'for there was none that cried but dogs'.

Today the statue of Cromwell — sword in one hand, Bible in the other — rightly enjoys pride of place outside the Houses of Parliament. But the father of the great English Revolution actually proved how little revolution England could take, inoculating us permanently against deposing monarchs, rule by armies or morality by decree. It is the measure of his achievement that there are more roads and streets in England named after Oliver Cromwell than anyone except Queen Victoria — and none in Ireland.

RABBI MANASSEH AND THE
RETURN OF THE JEWS

1655

MANASSEH BEN ISRAEL MADE IT HIS MIS-
sion to secure freedom of worship for his fellow Jews.
He was a rabbi living in Amsterdam during the years of the
English Commonwealth, and, like many in Europe, he was
fascinated by England's great experiment in the aftermath of
killing its king. He particularly pondered the burgeoning of
cults and religions that followed the Civil War, for Parliament's victorious Puritans had wasted no time in abolishing
the Church of England and its monopoly over worship.
Bishops, prayer books and compulsory churchgoing — all
the mechanisms of an established state religion — were

swept away: people were free to work out their own route to salvation.

'After the Bible was translated into English,' wrote the political theorist Thomas Hobbes, 'Everyman, nay, every boy and wench that could read English, thought they spoke with God Almighty and understood what he said.' An outspoken royalist, Hobbes had spent the Civil War in exile in Paris. There he gave maths lessons to Charles, the teenage Prince of Wales, while writing his great work of philosophy, *Leviathan*. Human life, said Hobbes, was 'solitary, poor, nasty, brutish and short'. In his opinion, humans needed a strong ruler — a Leviathan or giant — to impose order upon their unruly natures. A king was the obvious candidate, but England's King had been destroyed, and two years after Charles's execution the inquiring philosopher went bravely back to England to investigate life in the absence of the royal Leviathan.

Hobbes found the Commonwealth teeming with the new faiths, many with names that reflected their aims. The Levellers (see p. 195) were fighting for social equality; the Diggers prayed and campaigned for land reform; the Baptists favoured adult baptism; the Quakers trembled at the name of the Lord; the Ranters, for their part, believed that nothing human was wrong, permitting them to 'rant' — meaning to swear blasphemously — while also smoking and drinking and practising free love. The Muggletonians took their name from their spokesman Ludovicke Muggleton, who claimed to be one of the godly witnesses mentioned in the Book of Revelation; while the Fifth Monarchists derived their theories from Daniel's Old Testament dream: they interpreted the four beasts he saw as the four great empires of the ancient world, which were now being succeeded by a fifth, the reign of Christ — whose saints they were.

Hobbes threw up his hands at this bewildering array of creeds. These manifestly contradictory views of God confirmed his amoral and very post-modern view of life's essential chaos. But the Commonwealth's closest thing to Leviathan, Oliver Cromwell, rather welcomed the diversity. 'I had rather that Mahometanism were permitted amongst us,' he said, 'than that one of God's children should be persecuted.'

When the Diggers and Levellers had threatened property and public order immediately after the death of the King and again during the Protectorate, Cromwell had gone along with the army's suppression of their disorder. He expected his major generals to be stern in their enforcement of the new regime. But when it came to the faith inside a man's heart and head, he held firmly that freedom of worship was the right of 'the most mistaken Christian [who] should desire to live peaceably and quietly under you, [and] soberly and humbly desire to live a life of godliness and honesty'. Liberty of conscience was 'a natural right, and he that would have it ought to give it'.

This was the cue for Rabbi Manasseh Ben Israel. In 1654 he sent his son to see the Lord Protector, and the following year he left Amsterdam for London and was granted a personal audience. The Jews had been expelled from England three hundred and fifty years earlier by Edward I (see *Great Tales*, vol. 1, p. 174), and prejudice still lingered. Indeed, rumours of the letters the rabbi had been sending to Cromwell had prompted speculation that the Lord Protector might be planning to sell St Paul's to the Jews, to be turned into a synagogue: Christian merchants, it was feared, would be elbowed aside by ringleted Shylocks.

Cromwell was too clever to exacerbate such feeling with a formal decree or invitation of readmission to Jews. But he used his personal authority to make sure that they could now benefit from the toleration being enjoyed by other religious groups. In 1656 Jews started worshipping openly in their own synagogue in Creechurch Lane, near London's Aldgate, and within a few years there were thirty to forty Jewish families, mostly of Portuguese origin, operating in the capital as bankers and as dealers in gold and gemstones. The centuries of exclusion were over.

CHARLES II AND
THE ROYAL OAK

1660

IN SEPTEMBER 1651, KING CHARLES II CLIMBED
up a makeshift wooden ladder to hide in the branches of
a leafy oak tree near Boscobel House in Shropshire. His face
was blackened with soot scraped from inside a chimney and
his hair had been hastily cropped. Wearing the rough
breeches and shirt of a simple woodman, he carried enough
bread, cheese and beer to sustain him till nightfall. The
twenty-one-year-old, who had been claiming the English
throne since the execution of his father eighteen months
earlier, was on the run. The royalist army he had led down
from Scotland had been routed at Worcester two days earlier, and now the Roundhead search parties were scouring

the countryside. 'While we were in this tree,' he later re-called, 'we see soldiers going up and down in the thicket of the wood, searching for persons escaped, we seeing them, now and then, peeping out of the wood.'

In later life, Charles loved telling the story of his refuge in the Royal Oak — how sore his feet had felt in his badly fit-ting shoes and how he had actually spent most of his time in the tree asleep. Thirty years later he related the full story: on one occasion he had hidden in a barn behind mounds of corn and hay, on another the sound of galloping hooves had made him dive behind a hedge for cover.

Charles was a fugitive for no less than six weeks, first heading north from Worcester, then doubling back south, fi-nally making his escape to France from the little port of Shoreham in Sussex. Along the way he was sheltered by dozens of ordinary folk — millers, shepherds, farmers — as well as by prosperous landowners, many of them Catholics, who would hide him behind the panelling in their priest holes. There was a price of £1,000 on Charles's head, and the death penalty for anyone who helped him. But the King, as this young man already was in the eyes of most, would not be betrayed.

The Crown exercised an enduring hold on England's affec-tions. The many faults of Charles I were forgotten in the shock of what came to be seen as his martyrdom, and the succes-sion of republican experiments from Commonwealth to Pro-tectorate made a restoration of the monarchy seem the best guarantee of stability. But the death of Cromwell in Septem-ber 1658 did not immediately lead to the return of Charles II. Power rested with the thirty thousand officers and men of the Puritan army who were, for the most part, fiercely opposed to the return of the monarch, not to mention the 'popish' Church of England. The title of Protector had been taken over by Oliver's son Richard, and so long as the victors of the Civil War hung together it seemed likely that Charles would remain in exile. As his shrewd adviser Edward Hyde put it, for the monarchy to be restored, its enemies — Puritans, parliamentarians and soldiers — would have to become 'each other's executioners'.

It happened more quickly than anyone had imagined. Richard Cromwell was no leader — he lacked his father's sense of purpose and the very particular prestige that old 'Ironsides' had always enjoyed with his fellow-generals and other ranks too. After only seven months the army removed Richard, and May 1659 saw the return of the forty or so remaining members of the 'Rump' Parliament. This little band of veterans who had survived Pride's purge and dismissal by Oliver Cromwell could claim a distant, if slightly tortuous, legitimacy that went back, through all the travails of the Commonwealth and Civil Wars, to England's last full-scale elections in 1640. But they handled their comeback no more competently than their previous spell in power. By the end of 1659 they were again presiding over chaos, with taxes unpaid and rioters calling for proper elections.

Watching this slide into disorder was George Monck, commander of the English army occupying Scotland. Of solid Devon stock, the fifty-one-year-old Monck was a tough professional soldier, but he hated what he called the 'slavery of sword government' as fiercely as any civilian. In the closing days of the year he mobilised his forces at Coldstream, where they were stationed on the Scottish border, and started the march south. When he reached London in February 1660, he insisted that Parliament's deliberations could not continue without the participation of the MPs who had been excluded by Pride's purge and he finally put an end to the infamous Rump. London celebrated with revelling and barbecues. That night, 11 February, the streets smelt of roasting meat as rumps were turned on open-air spits in every corner of the city — thirty-one bonfires were counted on London Bridge alone.

Monck was now England's undisputed ruler, but he refused to make himself Lord Protector. Instead he opened negotiations with Charles II, whose little government-in-exile was gathered at Breda in Holland, and on 4 April 1660, Charles issued the Declaration of Breda, effectively his contract for restoration. Shrewdly heeding the advice of Edward Hyde, he kept his promises vague, placing his destiny in the hands of 'a free parliament'. Charles undertook to grant liberty to 'tender consciences' and a free pardon to all who had fought for Parliament — with the exception of the 'regicides' who had signed his father's death warrant. The army was promised settlement of all pay arrears in full.

The following month, the diarist and naval administrator Samuel Pepys joined Charles and his brother James, at Scheveningen near The Hague, on the ship that would bring them back to a triumphant reception in London. It was the Commonwealth's flagship the *Naseby*, named after the parliamentary victory in the Civil War, and after dinner its name was repainted — as the *Royal Charles*. England was royal again.

As sailors shinned up the rigging, setting the sails for England, Pepys fell into conversation with the tall, dark thirty-year-old who would shortly be crowned Charles II. Walking up and down the quarterdeck with him, the diarist was impressed. He found Charles 'very active and stirring . . . quite contrary to what I thought him to have been' — and scarcely able to believe quite how dramatically his fortunes had been transformed in a mere nine years. 'He fell into discourse of his escape from Worcester . . . where it made me ready to weep to hear the stories that he told of his difficulties that he had passed through.'

THE VILLAGE THAT
CHOSE TO DIE

1665

Xenopsylla cheopis

PLAGUE CAME TO ENGLAND WITH THE BLACK
Death in 1348, and it stayed. According to London's 'bills
of mortality', people died quite regularly from the infection,
which had ballooned to epidemic proportions in 1563, 1593,
1603, 1625 and 1636. The rich studied the bills of mortality as
a guide to their holiday plans. When the weekly plague rate
started rising, it was time for a trip to the country.

The Latin *plaga* means a blow or knock, and in those days
people often interpreted the erratic pattern of plague infec-
tions as punishing blows from an angry God. A more
earthly explanation was that poisonous vapours lurked beneath the earth's crust, symptom of a cosmic constipation

that could only be cured 'by expiring those Arsenical Fumes that have been retained so long in her bowels'.

Modern science remains baffled by the comings and goings of this deadly contagion. We know that bubonic plague is spread by infected fleas living on rats and humans. It is *not* spread from human to human by physical contact or even by human breath, except in the comparatively rare cases of pneumonic plague where the infection, having penetrated the lungs, is then breathed out by the sufferer in his or her brief remaining hours of painful life. The multiplication of rats and their fleas can be related to climactic factors — the rat flea *Xenopsylla cheopis* hibernates in frosty weather and flourishes at 20-25 degrees Celsius. But no one has convincingly connected particular conditions of heat or cold to the epidemic years — not least to September 1665, when plague hit England again with a vengeance. The bills of mortality mounted alarmingly — to seven thousand deaths a week by the end of the month — and the city streets sounded to the tolling of bells and the rumbling of plague carts as their drivers hooked up bodies left in doorways to convey them to the burial pits outside the city walls. Crosses were daubed on homes where infection had struck and their doors were boarded up, condemning those inside to almost certain death or — in just a few unexplained cases — to miraculous recovery.

Outside London, the plague spread wherever *X. cheopis* travelled, and it is thought to have reached the village of Eyam in Derbyshire that September in a box of tailor's samples and old clothing sent to Edward Cooper, a village trader. The clothes were damp on arrival, so Cooper's servant, George Vickers, placed them before the fire to dry. Within three days, a bluish-black plague-spot appeared on Vickers's chest, and he died the next day. Cooper followed him to the graveyard two weeks later, and by the end of October Eyam had suffered another twenty-six deaths. The mortality rate slowed during the hard Peak District winter to between four and nine a month, but with spring it rose again, and by midsummer 1666 over seventy of the village's 360 inhabitants had succumbed.

The old rector of Eyam, Thomas Stanley, had recently been ousted. A dissenter, he was one of the thousand or so Puritans who had refused to conform to the Church of England when, along with the monarchy, it had been restored six years earlier. So Stanley was deprived of his living, but he stayed on in Eyam, and seems to have collaborated with his young successor, the Revd William Mompesson, in face of the terrifying threat to their flock.

It was Mompesson, a married man with two children, who took the step that made Eyam famous — he urged his congregation to follow Jesus's words in the Gospel of St John: 'Greater love hath no man than this, that a man lay down his life for his friends.' Rather than fleeing the village and spreading the infection around the Peak District, argued the young rector, the community should stick together and help their fellow-men. This, clearly, was to risk their own lives in an act of extraordinary self-sacrifice. The congregation agreed, and for more than a year Eyam became effectively a huge plague house, shut off from the world. Their neighbours, meanwhile, who included the Earl of Devonshire at nearby Chatsworth, responded to their gesture by leaving food and other provisions at the outskirts of the village. Derbyshire was spared further plague, and Eyam paid the price, losing more than 260 inhabitants, some three-quarters of the population. Among the last to die was Mompesson's wife Catherine, who had gone from house to house during the outbreak, ministering to the sick.

The final burial took place on 11 October 1666, and Mompesson started assessing the damage. 'Our town has become a Golgotha, the place of a skull . . .' he wrote in November. 'I intend, God willing, to spend this week in seeing all woollen clothes fumed and purified . . .' Modern quarantine procedure suggests that this is the very first thing Eyam should have done. Had the fleas that were lurking in Edward Cooper's box of clothing been destroyed on day one, the villagers would have posed no threat to their neighbours. And even if the fleas had not been destroyed, those who left the village flealess could not have infected anyone they met.

In scientific terms, we can now say that the sacrifice of Eyam's villagers was probably unnecessary, and quite certainly counterproductive. By staying together they actually brought more humans, fleas and rats into close proximity, hugely increasing the mortality from a single source of infection. But if their lack of knowledge now seems a tragedy, does that invalidate the brave and selfless decision they took?

LONDON BURNING

1666

AT TWO O'CLOCK ON THE MORNING OF Sunday 2 September 1666, Thomas Farynor awoke to the smell of burning. Farynor bore the title of King's Baker — meaning that he baked ships' biscuits for the navy rather than bread for the King — and he lived above his bakery in Pudding Lane, not far from London Bridge. Dashing downstairs, he met with a blaze of such intensity that he snatched up his family and fled. Modern excavations have unearthed the carbonised remains of twenty tar barrels in the cellar below Pudding Lane, and it was probably their explosion that catapulted burning debris into the stables of the inn next door, setting fire to the hay piled up in the yard.

It had been a long hot summer. London's wood and wattle houses, roofed with straw, were tinderbox-dry, and a warm wind was blowing from the east. By three a.m. the city's fire-fighters were on hand, accompanied by the Lord Mayor Sir Thomas Bloodworth, tetchy at having had his sleep disturbed. He gave the conflagration a cursory glance, then returned to his bed. 'Pish!' he sniffed, 'a woman might piss it out!'

But while the Lord Mayor slept, the flames licked their way to the riverside, enveloping the wooden wharves and warehouses that were stacked to the rafters with merchandise waiting to burn. Tallow, oil, timber, coal — in no time an inferno was raging up the shoreline and had consumed a third of the houses on London Bridge. 'Rattle, rattle, rattle . . .' wrote one eyewitness, 'as if there had been a thousand iron chariots, beating together on the stones.' The fire was roaring along so fast that it caught any pigeons too slow to get out of its path, setting their feathers alight.

By Sunday lunchtime, Mayor Bloodworth's coarse complacency had turned to panic. Samuel Pepys found him sweating helplessly at the front line, a handkerchief tied round his neck. 'Lord, what can I do?' he cried. 'People will not obey me!'

Bloodworth's only recourse was the one reliable defence that the seventeenth century could offer against fire — to pull down blocks of houses to create firebreaks. But he found himself up against the fiercely protective instincts of some of the city's most powerful property owners, and it took royal intervention to get the firebreak policy under way. In fact, King Charles and his brother James were the fire-fighting heroes of that day, and of the three further days it took to bring the blaze under control. The King sent his Life Guards along to help, and the two brothers were soon out on the streets themselves, setting to with shovels and buckets of water. Working from five in the morning until nearly midnight, James came in for particular praise. 'If the Lord Mayor had done as much,' said one citizen, 'his example might have gone far towards saving the city.'

Thirteen thousand two hundred houses, 87 churches, and 44 merchant guild halls, along with the City's own Guildhall, Exchange, Custom House and the Bridewell Prison, were destroyed in the fire that started at Pudding Lane. For several nights the flames burned so brightly that they lit the horizon at Oxford, fifty miles away. One hundred thousand were made homeless — tent cities sprang up in the fields around the capital. And with no compensation available for rebuilding — at this date insurance existed only for ships — many were left destitute.

It was hardly surprising that a catastrophe of such magnitude should prompt a witch-hunt. When MPs gathered at the end of September they agreed to a man that papist saboteurs were to blame, and they set up a commission to prove it, solemnly gathering gossip about sinister French firework-makers and Catholic housewives from Ilford overheard predicting hot weather.

In fact, there is not the slightest evidence that the fire which started in Thomas Farynor's biscuit bakery in Pudding Lane in September 1666 was anything but an accident. And there was a certain half-heartedness in the Protestant attempts to pin the blame on the papists. Coupled with the 'blow' of the plague the previous year, people felt a depressing anxiety that the punishment might be the work of God himself — His judgement on a king and a monarchy that, in just a few years, had fallen sadly short of all that its restoration had promised.

TITUS OATES AND
THE POPISH PLOT

1678/9

KING CHARLES II WAS PROUD TO HAVE
fathered no less than fourteen illegitimate children. His
pursuit of pleasure summed up the spirit with which
Restoration England threw off the drab constraints of the
Puritan years. Strolling in the park with his knock-kneed,
floppy-eared spaniels, the 'Merry Monarch' privately believed in his divine right to rule as totally as his father
had, but unlike his father, Charles II masked his mission
with the common touch. Orange-seller turned actress Nell
Gwynne was the most popular of his many mistresses, famously turning jeers to cheers when anti-Catholic demon-

strators jostled her carriage. Red-haired Nelly leaned out of the window.'I am the *Protestant* whore!' she cried.

'King Charles II,' wrote John Evelyn, 'would doubtless have been an excellent prince had he been less addicted to women.' The King, explained Evelyn, was 'always in want to supply their immeasurable profusion'.

Women and wars drained the royal coffers. Under Charles, England's taxes rose to even higher levels than under the Commonwealth and Protectorate, but without the military triumphs that had made Cromwell's wars palatable. In June 1667 a marauding Dutch fleet entered the Thames estuary and sailed up the River Medway, where its fire ships destroyed half the English fleet. The Dutch cannon were clearly heard many miles away in fire-devastated London, while the newly renamed *Royal Charles* was captured and towed ignominiously back to Holland.

The humiliation in the Medway ended the Restoration honeymoon. Charles had been careful to avoid dissolving the 'Cavalier' Parliament that had been elected in the first joyously royalist flush of his return — at the end of every session he used the mechanism of prorogation (the temporary suspension of the Lords and Commons) to keep the Cavaliers returning. But these loyal merchants and country gentlemen distrusted the Roman Catholicism that permeated the royal court, and they disliked wasted taxes as much as the next man.

In 1670 Charles embarked on a disastrous course. Seeking extra funds that would diminish his reliance on Parliament, he made a secret pact with his cousin, the French

King Louis XIV. In return for a French pension that, in the event, would be paid intermittently for the rest of his reign, he agreed not only to restore the rights of English Catholics but also, when the moment was right, personally to acknowledge the Catholic faith in which he had been brought up by his devout French mother, Henrietta Maria.

The secret clauses were negotiated at Dover as part of a deal creating an Anglo-French alliance against the Dutch, and to camouflage his betrayal Charles appointed two of his ministers to negotiate a 'cover' Treaty of Dover — without the sell-out over Catholicism. But it was not long before suspicions of under-the-table dealings emerged, and when Charles went before Parliament in 1674 to swear there had been no secret clauses, it was observed that his hand shook.

The King's problems were intensified by the fact that, despite his profusion of bastard children, he had produced no legitimate heirs. His marriage to the Portuguese Catherine of Braganza remained obstinately childless, and though faithless to his spouse in so many ways, Charles refused to discard her. This handed the succession squarely to his brother James, Duke of York, who, unlike Charles, was not prepared to disguise his faith. In 1673 James had resigned his post as Lord High Admiral rather than denounce the doctrine of transubstantiation (see p. 102) as required by the Test Act, Parliament's attempt to exclude non-Anglicans from public office. Thus the heir to England's ultimate public office openly declared himself a Roman Catholic.

With the present King living a lie and his successor conjuring up the prospect of a re-enactment of the fires of Smithfield, it was small wonder that Protestant England felt under threat — and on 17 October 1678 came the event that seemed to justify their wildest fears. The body of Sir Edmund Berry Godfrey, a prominent London magistrate, was found face down in a ditch on Primrose Hill, run through with a sword. Godfrey had been a rare London hero of the plague year. He had stayed in the capital overseeing mass burials and prosecuting grave robbers, and shortly before his death, it now turned out, he had embarked on a still more heroic mission: he was investigating allegations of a sinister 'Popish Plot' to murder the King and place James on the throne.

The allegations had been laid before the magistrate by one Titus Oates, an oily and pompous con man of the cloth, who had been expelled from his school, two Cambridge colleges, his Church of England ministry, the navy, and two Catholic colleges in Europe for offences that ranged from drunkenness to sodomy — with an ongoing strand of perjury. Oates's tabloid tales of dagger-wielding Jesuit assassins might normally have commanded little credence, but the murder of Sir Edmund Berry Godfrey — which was never solved — gave his 'Popish Plot' a horrid plausibility. The magistrate's body was put on public display, and enterprising tradesfolk hawked 'Edmund Berry Godfrey' daggers to citizens newly concerned with self-defence. In the panic that followed, further informers came crawling out of the woodwork, leading to the prosecution of more than twelve hundred Catholics in London alone and the execution of twenty-four innocent men and women on charges of treason.

Parliamentarians and Puritans now saw a pressing need to exclude the King's popish brother from the succession, and the bitter battle to impose this 'exclusion' on Charles produced rudimentary political parties. Campaigning for exclusion was a 'country' alliance of Puritans, populists and old parliamentary diehards — derided by their opponents as 'Whiggamores', a term of abuse for Scottish Presbyterian outlaws. In response, the 'Whigs' denounced the 'court' party of High Anglicans and loyal monarchists as 'Tories' (from the Gaelic word *toraighe* — an Irish label for Catholic bandits).

Outlaws versus bandits, Whigs versus Tories: thus, in mutual insult, was born the British two-party political system. By the early 1680s the rival groupings were proudly proclaiming their names, printing manifestos, financing newspapers and choosing candidates. They even issued coloured rosettes — red for Tories and true blue for Whigs — and in this, the first of their many great confrontations, the Whigs managed to build up the larger majorities in the House of Commons.

But though the Whigs had the votes, they found themselves helpless in face of the King's prerogative powers, which were still essentially those enjoyed by Charles I — it was as if Commonwealth, Protectorate and Restoration had never been. Whenever the Whigs got close to passing a bill that would exclude James, his brother dissolved Parliament, and after three bitterly debated sessions and three dissolutions, the exclusion crisis ran out of steam. The fabrications of Titus Oates were exposed, and for the last five years of his reign Charles II was able to rule without Parliament.

The King's guiding principle had always been that he 'did not wish to go again on his travels', and through charm, deceit and a general unwillingness on the part of his subjects to fight another Civil War, he succeeded. Charles II never had to climb another oak tree or blacken his face with soot again. On his deathbed, he called for a priest and formally converted to the faith of his childhood. But as the Merry Monarch headed for his Catholic heaven, his farewell words paid due homage to his licentious past — 'Let not poor Nelly starve'.

MONMOUTH'S REBELLION
AND THE BLOODY ASSIZES

1685

JAMES, DUKE OF MONMOUTH, WAS CHARLES
II's eldest and favourite son, the product of his first serious love affair — in 1649, with Lucy Walter, an attractive,
dark-eyed Englishwoman living in Paris. This was the year
of Charles I's execution, and it was later recounted that
the nineteen-year-old prince, suddenly and tragically King-
in-exile, fell so deeply in love with Lucy that he secretly married her.

Charles always denied that Lucy was his legitimate wife,
but he showed great favour to his handsome firstborn, award-
ing him the dukedom — the highest rank of aristocracy —
when the boy was only fourteen, and arranging his marriage

to a rich heiress. Sixteen years later, in 1679, Charles entrusted him with the command of an English army sent to subdue Scottish rebels, and the thirty-year-old returned home a conquering hero.

As the exclusion crisis intensified, the Whigs embraced Monmouth as their candidate for the throne — here was a dashing 'Protestant Duke' to replace the popish James — and Monmouth threw himself into the part. He embarked on royal progresses, currying popular favour by taking part in village running races, and even touching scrofula sufferers for the King's Evil (see *Great Tales*, vol. 1, p. 81). But Charles was livid at this attempt by his charming but bastard son to subvert the line of lawful succession. He twice issued proclamations reasserting Monmouth's illegitimacy.

The transition of rule from Charles to James II in February 1685 was marked by a widespread acceptance — even a warmth — that had seemed impossible in the hysterical days of the Popish Plot. Without forswearing his Catholic loyalties, James pledged that he would 'undertake nothing against the religion [the Church of England] which is established by law', and most people gave him the benefit of the doubt. At the relatively advanced age of fifty-two, the new King cut a competent figure, reassuringly more serious and hardworking than his elder brother.

But Monmouth, in exile with his Whig clique in the Netherlands, totally misjudged the national mood. On 11 June that year he landed at the port of Lyme Regis in Dorset with just eighty-two supporters and equipment for a thousand more. Though his promises of toleration for dissenters drew the support of several thousand West Country artisans and labourers, the local gentry raised the militia against him, and the duke was soon taking refuge in the swamps of Sedgemoor where King Alfred had hidden from the Vikings eight hundred years earlier. Lacking Alfred's command of the terrain, however, Monmouth got lost in the mists during an attempted night attack, and as dawn broke on 6 July his men were cut to pieces.

Nine days later the 'Protestant Duke' was dead, executed in London despite grovelling to his victorious uncle and offering to turn Catholic in exchange for his life. It was a sorry betrayal of the Somerset dissenters who had signed up for what would prove the last popular rebellion in English history — and there was worse to come. Not content with the slaughter of Sedgemoor and the summary executions of those caught fleeing from the field, James insisted that a judicial commission headed by the Lord Chief Justice, George Jeffreys, should go down to the West Country to root out the last traces of revolt.

Travelling with four other judges and a public executioner, Jeffreys started his cull in Winchester, where Alice Lisle, the seventy-year-old widow of the regicide Sir John Lisle, was found guilty of harbouring a rebel and condemned to be burned at the stake. When Jeffreys suggested that she might plead to the King for mercy, Widow Lisle took his advice — and was spared burning to be beheaded in the marketplace. Moving on to Dorchester on 5 September, Jeffreys was annoyed to be confronted by a first batch of thirty suspects all pleading 'not guilty': he sentenced all but one of them to death. Then, in the interests of speed, he offered more lenient treatment to those pleading 'guilty'. Out of 233, only eighty were hanged.

By the time the work of the Bloody Assizes was finished, 480 men and women had been sentenced to death, 260 whipped or fined, and 850 transported to the colonies, where the profits from their sale were enjoyed by a syndicate that included James's wife, Mary of Modena. The tarred bodies and heads pickled in vinegar that Judge Jeffreys distributed around the gibbets of the West Country were less shocking to his contemporaries than they would be to subsequent generations. But his Bloody Assizes did raise questions about the new Catholic King, and how moderately he could be trusted to use his powers.

THE GLORIOUS INVASION

1688-9

THOSE WHO DISLIKED ENGLAND HAVING AN openly Catholic monarch took comfort from the thought that James II could not live for ever. The King was comparatively old by seventeenth-century standards — in October 1687 he turned fifty-four, the age at which his brother had died — and his immediate heirs, his daughters Mary (twenty-five) and Anne (twenty-three), were both staunch Protestants. Mary, indeed, was married to the Dutch Protestant hero William of Orange, who had his own place in the English succession (see family tree p. xi), and who was leading Holland's battle against the empire-building ambitions of Catholic France. (The 'Orange' in William's title referred to the French town near Avignon that had once belonged to his family.)

Mary and Anne were the surviving offspring of James's first marriage, to Anne Hyde, the daughter of Charles II's adviser in exile, Edward Hyde. Following her death in 1671 James had married an Italian Catholic, Mary, daughter of the Duke of Modena, and the couple had worked hard to produce a Catholic heir — Mary of Modena went through ten pregnancies in the decade 1674-84. But these had produced five stillbirths and five who died in infancy, so by the time James II came to the throne, Protestants could safely feel that his wife's reproductive capacity posed them no threat.

They had not reckoned on the visits that Queen Mary started making to the ancient city of Bath with its curative spa waters, and just before Christmas 1687 came alarming news — the Bath fertility treatment had worked. Mary of Modena was pregnant for an eleventh time, and early in June 1688, she gave birth to a healthy baby boy. Named James and styled Prince of Wales, this new arrival displaced his Protestant sisters from the succession and suddenly offered England the prospect of a Catholic Stuart monarchy in perpetuity.

English Protestants refused to believe James's luck — the birth had to be a fake. Pamphlets were rushed out asserting that the strapping baby was a miller's son, smuggled into the royal bed in a long-handled warming-pan. Vivid graphic images circulated, showing how the deception must have been carried out, and it was in vain that the King marshalled a chamberful of respected Protestant witnesses to swear to the genuineness of the birth. The story of the 'baby in the warming-pan' proved one of history's most persuasive conspiracy theories.

After three years on the throne, James was arousing widespread suspicion. He had promised not to undermine the established Church, but evidence was mounting that his true purpose was to steer England back towards Rome. By March 1688 a succession of moves favouring Catholics and dissenters had ousted more than twelve hundred members of the Church of England from public office, and though James claimed to be unbiased, even his own family dismissed as a popish ploy his recently cultivated tolerance towards nonconformists. 'Things are come to that pass now,' wrote his daughter Anne from London to her elder sister in Holland, 'that if they go on much longer, I believe no Protestant will be able to live.'

James was knocking the stilts from under his own conservative powerbase. The Anglican Tory squires who had welcomed his accession were incensed to see their own kind being replaced on the magistrates' benches by papists and Puritans — and seriously alarmed when Catholics were given positions of command in the King's rapidly growing standing army. On 30 June, less than three weeks after the birth of the Prince of Wales, seven senior peers, their signatures in code, sent a secret invitation to Mary's husband William of Orange to come over to England.

William needed no prompting. He spent that summer preparing an army and an invasion fleet — 463 vessels and forty thousand troops — along with sixty thousand pamphlets to explain his purpose. He did not intend to seize the crown, he said. His expedition was 'intended for no other design, but to have a free and lawful parliament assembled as soon as possible' — and to inquire, among other matters, 'into the birth of the pretended Prince of Wales'.

William's Dutch and German invasion force was larger than Philip of Spain had assembled for the Armada of 1588, but when the Dutch prince landed in Torbay in November a hundred years later, his success was by no means guaranteed. His foreign mercenaries might well have it in them to defeat the twenty-thousand-strong English army that was blocking their way to London. But shedding English blood would have ruined William's claim to be acting in English interests, and would also have exposed his basic reason for invading England — he wanted England's military might on Holland's side in its ongoing battle against Louis XIV.

William was fortunate that, at the moment of confrontation, James lost his nerve. Though debilitated by nosebleeds and insomnia, the King made haste to join his army on Salisbury Plain — only to return abruptly to London, where he discovered that his daughter Anne had deserted and joined the cause of her sister and brother-in-law. Lear-like, James raged against the perfidy of his daughters. Having sent the Queen and the Prince of Wales ahead of him, he fled Whitehall on 11 December by a secret passage, throwing the Great Seal of England petulantly into the Thames as he left.

At this point a band of overzealous Kent fishermen spoiled the plot. They arrested James at Faversham and dispatched him back to London — to William's embarrassed fury. The Dutch prince promptly returned his father-in-law to Kent, with an escort briefed to look the other way when they got the King to Rochester. At the second attempt, James made good his escape.

Six weeks later, on 13 February 1689, William and Mary accepted the English crown as joint sovereigns in return for their agreement to the passing by Parliament of a 'Bill of Rights' — a mutually convenient deal that has gone down in history as 'the Glorious Revolution'. This is generally taken to mean that 1688/9 marked the inauguration of England's constitutional monarchy — the moment when Parliament finally codified the control over the Crown that it had won in the Civil War, but had failed to secure in the reigns of Charles II and James II.

In fact, the Bill of Rights of 1689 said very little about the rights of individuals, and it would be more than a century before England's monarchy could truly be called 'constitutional'. In the horse-trading with Parliament that followed James II's effective abdication, the hard-headed William coolly defended his royal prerogatives, retaining his right to select his own ministers and to control the length of parliamentary sessions. Revolution? The year 1688/9 witnessed nothing so grass-roots or drastic in England — though from William's point of view his invasion had certainly enjoyed a glorious outcome.

ISAAC NEWTON AND THE
PRINCIPLES OF THE UNIVERSE

1687

ISAAC NEWTON WAS BORN IN THE LINCOLN-shire village of Woolsthorpe in 1642, the year that England's Civil War began. A small and sickly baby, he had an unhappy childhood, discarded by his widowed mother at the age of three when she remarried a rich clergyman who had no time for Isaac. But a kindly uncle helped him to school in the nearby market town of Grantham, and in 1661 the nineteen-year-old won admission to Trinity College, Cambridge.

Newton was not an outstanding student. But in 1665 the plague came to Cambridge, the students were sent home, and it was back in Woolsthorpe that he experienced the revelation he loved to recount in later life. Sitting in the shade of an apple tree one day, he watched an apple drop to the ground. 'Why should this apple always invariably fall to the earth in a perpendicular line?' he remembered thinking. 'Why should it not fall upwards, sideways, or obliquely?'

Newton did not publish his ideas about the law of gravity for another twenty years, and some have suggested that his subsequent description of his famous Eureka moment was nothing more than an exercise in myth-making. But Isaac had come up with another big idea during his plague-enforced gap year at Woolsthorpe, and it is not surprising that falling apples should take a back seat while he explored this equally intriguing — and literally dazzling — phenomenon: the structure of light. 'In the beginning of the year 1666 . . .' he later wrote, 'I procured me a triangular glass prism, to try therewith the celebrated phenomena of colours . . . Having darkened my chamber, and made a small hole in my window shuts [shutters] to let in a convenient quantity of the sun's light, I placed my prism at his entrance that it might be thereby refracted to the opposite wall.'

The prevailing theory at this time was that a prism produced colours by staining, or dyeing, the light that passed through it. But in his study at Woolsthorpe, where we can see today exactly where the twenty-five-year-old boffin played with the colours of the rainbow, Newton set up a second prism. If each prism coloured the light, the hues should have deepened as they passed through the second refraction. In fact, they returned to being bright and clear — Newton had put white light's component colours back together again.

This was the discovery that made his name. In 1672 he

was invited to publish his findings by the Royal Society of London for Improving Knowledge. This fellowship of inquiring minds had started life in Oxford and London during the Civil War when, lacking a fixed base, they called themselves the 'Invisible College'. Science was one of Charles II's more constructive interests, and in 1662 he had chartered the 'Invisible College' as the Royal Society, bestowing his patronage on the meeting and mingling of some extraordinary minds: Robert Boyle was working on the definition of chemical elements, together with the density, pressure and behaviour of gases; Robert Hooke was publicising the hidden world revealed by the microscope; Edmund Halley was investigating the movement of heavenly bodies like comets; and Christopher Wren, surveying the almost limitless architectural opportunities offered by fire-devastated London, was formulating a fresh vision of the structures required by city living.

Immediately elected a Fellow of the Royal Society for his work on 'opticks', Isaac Newton did not, in fact, get on very well with this illustrious fraternity. His troubled childhood had left him a solitary character, untrusting and morose. But it was a gathering of three more sociable Fellows that prompted the publication of his greatest work. Sitting in one of London's newly fashionable coffee houses one day in 1684, Halley, Wren and Hooke fell to discussing how to describe the movements of the planets, and shortly afterwards Halley visited Newton to put the question to him. Newton replied without hesitation: the planets moved in an ellipse. He had worked it out years earlier, he said, and when Halley asked to see his calculations, Newton promised to write them out for him.

The result was his *Principia Mathematica*, often described as the most important book in the history of science. In it Newton set out his three laws of motion, the second of these explaining the power of gravity and how it determined the motion of the planets and their moons, the movement of the tides and the apparently eccentric behaviour of comets. Halley used Newton's calculations to predict the course of the comet that would make him famous — Halley's Comet, which passed over England in 1682 and which he linked to reports of previous comet sightings in 1456, 1531 and 1607.

Having prompted Newton to write the *Principia*, it was Halley who extracted the manuscript from him, paid with his own money for its printing, and acted as its chief publicist, preparing reader-friendly summaries of Newton's often severely complicated ideas. Newton himself expressed his thoughts so dourly that students often avoided his lectures at Cambridge, and he spent his time 'lecturing to the walls'.

Today we see Isaac Newton as a pioneering scientist and the father of physics. In fact, the terms 'scientist' and 'physics' did not exist in his lifetime. Newton devoted long years of research to the ancient mysteries of alchemy and how base metals could be turned into gold. The modern scientists and historians involved in the 'Newton Project', a venture that will put all his ten million or so words on to the World Wide Web, report that more than a million of those words are devoted to alchemy, and another four million to lurid biblical prophecy — and particularly to the book of Revelation: the Whore of Babylon, the nature of the two-horned and ten-horned beasts and the Four Horsemen of the Apocalypse.

Yet between the lines of this ancient-sounding discourse

lurks a radical and forward-thinking vision. Newton eagerly awaits the moment when 'the Word of God makes war with ye Beasts & Kings of ye earth' to create a 'new heaven, new earth & new Jerusalem'. This man, born with the Civil War and producing his master work in the years when the absolutist Stuart monarchy finally collapsed, is rightly identified with modernity. He prepared the brief by which Cambridge University would defend its independence against King James II, and in 1689 he was elected to the Parliament that put William and Mary on the throne.

More important, his explanation of how the universe operated by logical mechanical laws was to cause a profound alteration in human thought. The work of Newton, Halley, Hooke and their contemporaries upended the very basis of philosophy and human inquiry, making once divine areas the province of their own earthly research. All things were possible. Reason, logic and deduction would replace blind faith. Old ideas were questioned. New ideas were explored. No longer did God reside in the heavens; he existed in your mind if you could find him there — a transformation in thinking that truly was a glorious revolution.

BIBLIOGRAPHY AND
SOURCE NOTES

The excellent general histories of Britain by Norman Davies, Simon Schama, Roy Strong, Michael Wood and others were set out in the bibliography to the previous volume of *Great Tales*. For the fifteenth, sixteenth and seventeenth centuries they are joined by:

Brigden, Susan, *New Worlds, Lost Worlds: The Rule of the Tudors, 1485-1603* (London, Penguin Books), 2000.

Guy, John, *Tudor England* (Oxford, Oxford University Press), 1988.

Haigh, Christopher, *English Reformations: Religion, Politics and Society under the Tudors* (Oxford, Oxford University Press), 1993.

Kishlansky, Mark, *A Monarchy Transformed: Britain 1603-1714* (London, Penguin Books), 1996.

Saul, Nigel (ed.), *The Oxford Illustrated History of Medieval England* (Oxford, Oxford University Press), 1997.

For a wide range of original documents, some in facsimile and all usually in translation, visit the following:

www.bl.com
www.fordham.edu/halsall

www.history.ac.uk/iht/resources/index.html
www.library.rdg.ac.uk/home.html
eebo.chadwyck.com/home

This last excellent website, Early English Books Online, is set up for institutions — your local library can apply for a free trial — but not individuals. You can find a backdoors way in, however, if you go to the interface supplied by the University of Michigan on www.hti.umich.edu/e/eebodemo/.

FURTHER READING AND PLACES TO VISIT

1387: *Geoffrey Chaucer and the Mother Tongue*

You can visit Chaucer's grave in Westminster Abbey, the memorial that inspired Poets' Corner. To read the very earliest editions of *The Canterbury Tales* as printed by William Caxton in the 1470s and 1480s, visit the British Library website, www.bl.uk/treasures/caxton/homepage.html — and for a wonderfully bawdy modern English version, read the classic translation by Nevill Coghill.

Coghill, Nevill, *The Canterbury Tales* (Harmondsworth, Penguin Books), 1951.

1399: *The Deposing of King Richard II*

Nigel Saul has written the definitive biography. Christopher Given Wilson has pulled together the contemporary sources.

Given Wilson, Christopher (ed.), *Chronicles of the Revolution, 1397–1400: The Reign of Richard II* (Manchester, Manchester University Press), 1993.
Saul, Nigel, *Richard II* (London, Yale University Press), 1997.

1399: 'Turn Again, Dick Whittington!'

For an evocative flavour of Whittington's London, visit the medieval gallery at the Museum of London, or its website: www. museumoflondon.org.uk.

1399: Henry IV and His Extra-virgin Oil

A recent academic conference has assembled the latest research and thinking on this enigmatic king.

Dodd, Gwilym, and Biggs, Douglas, *Henry IV: The Establishment of the Regime, 1399-1406* (York, Medieval Press), 2003.

1415: We Happy Few — the Battle of Azincourt

The two English films of *Henry V* by the Shakespearian giants of their respective generations are regularly rerun on television. Laurence Olivier's sun-filled idyll was shot in neutral Ireland during World War II, with the Irish army playing the bowmen of England. Kenneth Branagh's 1989 version presents, surely in deliberate contrast, a dark, brooding and rain-drenched interpretation.

1429: Joan of Arc, the Maid of Orleans

Marina Warner has written the definitive interpretation; George Bernard Shaw, the classic play. For transcriptions of Joan's trial, visit: archive.joan-of-arc.org.

Warner, Marina, *Joan of Arc, the Image of Female Heroism* (London, Weidenfeld & Nicolson), 1981.

1440: A 'Prompter for Little Ones'

Nicholas Orme's playful and original book is the inspiration for this chapter. The metal toys uncovered by Tony Pilson and the Mud Larks are exhibited in the medieval galleries at the Museum of London: www. museumoflondon.org.uk.

Orme, Nicholas, *Medieval Children* (London, Yale University Press), 2001.

1422–61, 1470–1: *House of Lancaster: the Two Reigns of Henry VI*

David Starkey's rereading of the 'Royal Book' of court etiquette has cast a new light on the supposed shabbiness of Henry VI. The Paston Letters, England's earliest set of family correspondence, provides a human picture of how the wars disturbed — and did not disturb — ordinary life. To get the flavour of one conflict, visit www.bloreheath.org, which walks you round the site of the 1459 battle. Eagle Media's DVD (emdv354) has preserved the History Channel's excellent series 'The Wars of the Roses'.

The original manuscripts of the Paston Letters are in the British Library (Catalogue nos. 27443-58, 34888-9, 43488-91, 39848-9, 36988, 33597, 45099), but you can read them online in several versions from the Old English to the modern abridged edition on various electronic libraries most easily accessed from www.google.com (because individual addresses tend to be long and change frequently). The University of Virginia's online library at www.lib.virginia.edu has all 421 letters or 1380 kilobytes' worth!

Starkey, David, 'Henry VI's Old Blue Gown', *The Court Historian*, vol. 4.1 (April 1999).

1432–85: *The House of Theodore*

Knowing that Pembrokeshire is Tudor country gives an extra dimension to visiting this south-west corner of Wales. Henry VII was born inside the dramatic thirteenth-century curtain walls of Pembroke Castle, www.pembrokecastle.co.uk, ten miles from Milford Haven where he landed in 1485 to claim the throne.

1461–70, 1471–83: *House of York: Edward IV, Merchant King*

Warwick Castle, the home of Warwick the Kingmaker, who made and was then unmade by Edward IV, was recently voted

Britain's most popular castle, ahead of the Tower of London. With its gardens landscaped by 'Capability' Brown in a later century, it is today impressively maintained by Madame Tussaud's: www.warwick-castle.co.uk.

Seward, Desmond, *The Wars of the Roses* (London, Robinson), 1995.

1474: William Caxton

Caxton is buried within yards of the site of his printing press, in St Margaret's, the little church that is so often overlooked in the shadow of Westminster Abbey. Along with his edition of *The Canterbury Tales*, the British Library has digitised a number of his works on www.bl.uk. To read his charming, often eccentric, publisher's prefaces, visit www.bartleby.com.

Painter, George, *William Caxton: A Quincentenary Biography of England's First Printer* (London, Chatto & Windus), 1976.

1483: Whodunit? The Princes in the Tower

The little princes were lodged by their uncle in the relatively luxurious royal apartments of the Tower. Visit the dungeons and watch the water come creeping under Traitors' Gate to enjoy the sinister chill of this fortress, prison, and high-class beheading place: www.hrp.org.uk. Dockray presents the contemporary evidence on the mystery, so you can make up your own mind.

Dockray, Keith, *Richard II: A Source Book* (Stroud, Sutton), 1997.

1484: The Cat and the Rat

'Now is the winter of our discontent . . .' Laurence Olivier's 1955 film portrayal of Richard III is the ultimate version of Shakespeare's crookback baddie. It might seem strange that the fullest and fairest account of this film is to be found on www.r3.org, the website of the Richard III Society, founded to clear and glorify the King's name. But that is the nature of this deservedly thriving association of historical enthusiasts.

1485: *The Battle of Bosworth Field*

This account of the Battle of Bosworth is based on the recent book by Michael K. Jones. Virginia Henderson examines the legend of the Tudor Rose in her article on Henry VII's chapel in Westminster Abbey, while Illuminata's definitive compendium on heraldic badges contains all you could possibly need to know about symbolic roses, Tudor and otherwise.

Henderson, Virginia, 'Retrieving the "Crown in the Hawthorn Bush": the origins of the badges of Henry VII', in *Traditions and Transformations in Late Medieval England*, ed. Douglas Biggs, Sharon D. Michalove and A. Compton Reeves (Leiden, Brill), 2002.

Jones, Michael K., *Bosworth 1485* (Stroud, Tempus), 2002.

Siddons, Michael Powell, *Heraldic Badges of England and Wales* (London, Illuminata Publishers for the Society of Antiquaries of London), 2005.

1486-99: *Double Trouble*

Again, www.r3.org, the website dedicated to his bitterest enemy, contains the most comprehensive and the latest material on Henry VII, and it is difficult not to recommend another visit to Westminster Abbey to view Henry's eerily lifelike death mask in the museum in the corner of the Cloisters.

1497: *Fish 'n' Ships*

www.matthew.co.uk relates the recent recreation of Cabot's historic voyage of exploration and the building of the modern replica Matthew, which can be visited in Bristol and, on Tuesday and Thursday evenings, cruised upon in the still waters of Bristol Harbour.

Pope, Peter E., *The Many Landfalls of John Cabot* (Toronto, University of Toronto Press), 1976.

1500: *Fork In, Fork Out*

Stanley Chrimes wrote the classic biography. Thompson's collection of essays re-evaluates the idea that Henry was a 'new' and non-medieval monarch.

Chrimes, Stanley B., *Henry VII* (New Haven, Yale University Press), 1999

Thompson, B. (ed.), *The Reign of Henry VII* (Stanford, Stanford University Press), 1995.

1509-33: *King Henry VIII's 'Great Matter'*

Built by Thomas Wolsey, Hampton Court breathes the grandiose spirit of its founder and, even more, that of the man who confiscated it from the cardinal, Henry VIII. The King enjoyed three honeymoons here, could entertain five hundred diners at one sitting, and worked up a sweat in the 'real' tennis court. In the garden is the famous maze. www.hrp.org.uk.

Thurley, Simon, *Hampton Court: A Social and Architectural History* (London, Yale University Press), 2003.

1525: *'Let There Be Light' — William Tyndale and the English Bible*

This account is largely based upon Brian Moynahan's revealing and passionate book.

Moynahan, Brian, *William Tyndale: If God Spare My Life* (London, Little, Brown), 2002.

1535: *Thomas More and His Wonderful 'No-Place'*

To read the complete text of Utopia visit the electronic library of Fordham University that contains so many wonderful original sources: www.fordham.edu/halsall/mod/thomasmore-utopia.html. Thomas More himself is buried in two places: his body in the Tower of London, and his head, retrieved by his devoted daughter Margaret Roper, in the Roper Vault at St Dunstan's Church, Canterbury.

1533–7: *Divorced, Beheaded, Died . . .*

Scarisbrick and Starkey share the honours in the large and distinguished field of those who have written about Henry VIII, his wives and his world.

Scarisbrick, J. J., *Henry VIII* (London, Eyre & Spottiswoode), 1968.
Starkey, David, *Six Wives: The Queens of Henry VIII* (London, Chatto & Windus), 2003.

1536: *The Pilgrimage of Grace*

In recent years the work of Eamon Duffy, Christopher Haigh and Diarmaid MacCulloch has done honour to the strength of traditional Catholic faith and practice in sixteenth-century England. They have shown how the Reformation did not so much reform as re-form — and in a variety of complex ways.

Duffy, Eamon, *The Stripping of the Altars: Traditional Religion in England c.1400–c.1580* (London, Yale University Press), 1992.
Haigh, Christopher (ed.), *The English Reformation Revised* (Cambridge, Cambridge University Press), 1987.
MacCulloch, Diarmaid, *Reformation: Europe's House Divided 1490–1700* (London, Penguin Books), 2004.

1539–47: *. . . Divorced, Beheaded, Survived*

Henry VIII is buried in the centre of the nave in St George's Chapel, Windsor, in the company of the wife for whom he overturned his country and who bore him the healthy male heir he desired so much. www.royal.gov.uk.

1547–53: *Boy King — Edward VI, 'The Godly Imp'*

Some grammar schools apart, there are few Tudor remnants dating from the boy king's short reign — and, sadly, an almost endless catalogue of Christian art was destroyed by the whitewash brush and the plundering fingers of those who 'purified' the Church in his name. Jordan's two-volume work is the best survey of the reign.

Jordan, W. K., vol. 1, *Edward VI: The Young King;* vol. 2, *Edward VI: The Threshold of Power* (London, George Allen & Unwin), 1968, 1970.

1553: Lady Jane Grey — the Nine-day Queen

Jane Grey spent her youth in Sudeley Castle at Winchcombe near Cheltenham in Gloucestershire, where Henry VIII's last wife, Catherine Parr, lies buried. In the Civil War it was for a time the headquarters of the dashing Prince Rupert. www.sudeleycastle.co.uk.

1553–8: Bloody Mary and the Fires of Smithfield

If one man created the legend of Bloody Mary, it was John Foxe, who painstakingly compiled the stories of her victims and brought them together in his *Book of Martyrs* — probably the bestselling book of the sixteenth-century and, arguably, the most influential. For the complete text visit www.ccel.org/f/foxe. Jasper Ridley's lucid modern account is largely based on Foxe.

Ridley, Jasper, *Bloody Mary's Martyrs* (London, Constable), 2001.

1557: Robert Recorde and His Intelligence Sharpener

The School of Mathematics and Statistics at Scotland's University of St Andrews has produced an excellent account of Recorde's life and work on: www-gap.dcs.st-and.ac. You can find the details of his horseshoe brain-teaser in Adam Hart-Davis's book:

Hart-Davis, Adam, *What the Tudors and Stuarts Did for Us* (London, Boxtree), 2002.

1559: Elizabeth — Queen of Hearts

David Starkey concentrates on the early years of Elizabeth. Christopher Haigh's 'profile in power' is the best condensed analysis of her life.

Haigh, Christopher, *Elizabeth I* (London, Longman), 1988.
Starkey, David, *Elizabeth* (London, Chatto & Windus), 2000.

1571: *That's Entertainment*
The contemporary descriptions in this chapter come from Liza Picard's brilliant evocation. If you can't visit the Globe in Southwark, you can enjoy Tom Stoppard's whimsical but scenically accurate *Shakespeare in Love*, now on DVD.

Picard, Liza, *Elizabeth's London: Everyday Life in Elizabethan London* (Weidenfeld & Nicolson), 2003.

1585: *Sir Walter Ralegh and the Lost Colony*
Ralegh once owned Sherborne Castle in Dorset, though there is not much left of it today after Oliver Cromwell's Civil War siege: www.sherbornecastle.com. And, in the spirit of Sir Walter himself, let me not forget to mention my own biography of the great adventurer, happily still in print.

Lacey, Robert, *Sir Walter Ralegh* (London, Phoenix Press), 2000.

1560-87: *Mary Queen of Scots*
Inns and castles where Mary Queen of Scots is said to have stayed are almost as numerous as those that boast 'Queen Elizabeth Slept Here'. Tutbury overlooks the Dove Valley in Staffordshire: tel.: 01283 812129. Nothing much remains of Fotheringhay on the River Nene near Oundle in Northamptonshire where she was executed, but nearby is the beautiful fifteenth-century church of St Mary and All Saints. Antonia Fraser's biography is definitive.

Fraser, Antonia, *Mary Queen of Scots* (London, Weidenfeld & Nicolson), 1969.

1588: *Sir Francis Drake and the Spanish Armada*
Drake lived at Buckland Abbey, eleven miles north of Plymouth. This beautiful thirteenth-century Cistercian monastery had been

spared destruction in the Dissolution when Henry VIII granted it to Sir Richard Grenville, whose grandson Richard, himself a naval hero, sold it to Sir Francis. Tel.: 01822 853607.

Cummings, John, *Francis Drake: The Lives of a Hero* (London, Weidenfeld & Nicolson), 1995.

1592: *Sir John's Jakes*
Named in honour of the modern populariser of the water closet, www.thomas-crapper.com graphically sets out the tale of sewage through the ages in more detail than most would consider strictly necessary. Again, Adam Hart-Davis provides a lively and intelligent summary.

Hart-Davis, Adam, *What the Tudors and Stuarts Did for Us* (London, Boxtree), 2002.

1603: *By Time Surprised*
Outliving three husbands, that other Elizabeth, Bess of Hardwick, Countess of Shrewsbury, built up a fortune that she devoted to building the redoubtable Hardwick Hall, near Chesterfield in Derbyshire. Tel.: 01246 850430. Mercifully spared the 'improvements' of later generations, it is a remarkably vivid and accurate example of a great Elizabethan country house.

1605: 5/11: *England's First Terrorist*
The cellar where Guy Fawkes stacked his gunpowder was destroyed in the fire of 1834 that devastated the medieval Houses of Parliament, but thanks to the Tradescants you can still see the lantern Guy Fawkes carried in 1605 in the Ashmolean Museum, Oxford.

Fraser, Antonia, *The Gunpowder Plot: Terror and Faith in 1605* (London, Weidenfeld & Nicolson), 1996.

1611: King James's 'Authentical' Bible
James VI and I's own prolific writings have been skilfully edited by Rhodes, Richards and Marshall. McGrath tells the story of the Bible he inspired.

McGrath, Alister, *In the Beginning: The Story of the King James Bible* (London, Hodder & Stoughton), 2001.

Rhodes, Neil, Richards, Jennifer, and Marshall, Joseph, *King James VI and I: Selected Writings* (Aldershot, Ashgate), 2003.

1616: 'Spoilt Child' and the Pilgrim Fathers
The sentimental Disney cartoon film Pocahontas enraged her descendants, who set out their objections on their website: www. powhatan. org. The best source on the Pilgrim Fathers remains William Bradford's first-hand account which is extracted, along with many other original documents, on the excellent www.mayflowerhistory.com.

Bradford, William (ed. S. E. Morison), *Of Plymouth Plantation 1620-47* (New York, Alfred A. Knopf), 1954.

1622: The Ark of the John Tradescants
The Tradescants, father and son, are buried in the beautiful St Mary-at-Lambeth, just across the Thames from the House of Commons. The church was saved from destruction in 1977 by the Tradescant Trust, who turned it into the world's first Museum of Garden History, complete with its own replica seventeenth-century knot garden of miniature box trees. www. museumgardenhistory. org.

Leith-Ross, Prudence, *The John Tradescants* (London, Peter Owen), 1984.

1629: God's Lieutenant in Earth
Charles I's cradle can be seen at Hatfield House in Hertfordshire where Elizabeth I, a virtual prisoner, was brought the news that

her sister Mary had died and she had become Queen. The Tudor building was largely torn down and we see Hatfield today as it was rebuilt in the reign of James I by Robert Cecil. Tel.: 01707 287010.

1642: 'All My Birds Have Flown'

It is difficult to better C. V. Wedgwood's classic account of this episode. Tristram Hunt movingly brings together the voices of the time.

Hunt, Tristram, *The English Civil War at First Hand* (London, Phoenix), 2003.

Wedgwood, C. V., *The King's War* (London, HarperCollins), 1955.

1642-8: Roundheads v. Cavaliers

No study of the Civil War can omit the inspired and seminal work of Christopher Hill. Royle shows the impact of the wars on Scotland and Ireland. Blair Worden brilliantly shows how the Civil Wars have been fought through the subsequent centuries.

Hill, Christopher, *Puritanism and Revolution: Studies in Interpretation of the English Revolution of the Seventeenth Century* (London, Secker & Warburg), 1958.

Royle, Trevor, *The Wars of the Three Kingdoms 1638-1660* (London, Little, Brown), 2004.

Worden, Blair, *Roundhead Reputations Ltd: The English Civil Wars and the Passions of Posterity* (London, Penguin Books), 2001.

1649: Behold the Head of a Traitor!

The magnificent Banqueting House from which Charles I walked to his execution still stands opposite Horse Guards Parade in Whitehall. Designed by Inigo Jones as a setting for the plays and pageants of Ben Jonson, it is decorated with ceiling panels that illustrate Charles's disastrous theories on the nature of kingship: one tableau shows James I rising to heaven after his death like a latter-day Christ, to take his place among the immortals. www.hrp.org.

1653: 'Take Away This Bauble!'

The remains of Oliver Cromwell, like those of the other regicides, were dug up and dismembered after the Restoration. His rotting head was set on a pole outside Westminster Hall for a quarter of a century. But you can see his death mask, warts and all, in the Museum of London, www.museumoflondon.org.uk, and you can visit the house where he lived from 1636 to 1647 in St Mary's Street, Ely. Tel.: 01353 662062.

Hill, Christopher, *God's Englishman: Oliver Cromwell and the English Revolution* (London, Weidenfeld & Nicolson), 1970.

Morrill, John (ed.), *Oliver Cromwell and the English Revolution* (London, Longman), 1990.

1655: Rabbi Manasseh and the Return of the Jews

The dark oak benches from the Creechurch Lane synagogue, which opened in 1656, were moved in 1701 to the Spanish and Portuguese Synagogue in Bevis Marks Street, now Britain's oldest synagogue. Built by a Quaker, the exterior resembles a non-conformist chapel, while the interior reflects the influence of Sir Christopher Wren. Tel.: 020 7626 1274.

1660: Charles II and the Royal Oak

Richard Ollard colourfully recreates Charles II's adventures after the Battle of Worcester — and we are now entering the age of the great diarists, whom Liza Picard quotes along with a host of other contemporary sources in her charming and intimate-feeling social history.

Bowle, John (ed.), *The Diary of John Evelyn* (Oxford, Oxford University Press), 1983.

Latham, R. (ed.), *The Shorter Pepys* (London, Bell & Hyman), 1985.

Ollard, Richard, *The Escape of Charles II* (London, Constable), 1986.

Picard, Liza, *Restoration London* (London, Weidenfeld & Nicolson), 2001.

1665: The Village That Chose to Die

Every year on Plague Sunday (the last Sunday in August) the modern inhabitants of Eyam hold an outdoor service to commemorate the heroic sacrifice of their predecessors. In 2000, Eyam's enterprising little museum was awarded the Museum of the Year Shoestring Award. www.eyammuseum.demon.co.uk. The Folio Society has recently republished Walter George Bell's classic account of the plague year.

Bell, Walter George, *The Great Plague in London* (London, Folio Society), 2001.

1666: London Burning

The tragedy of the Great Fire produced the finest building of the seventeenth century, and arguably England's finest building ever. 'Lector, Si Monumentum Requeris, Circumspice' ('Reader, if you seek a monument, then look around you') runs Sir Christopher Wren's inscription beneath the dome of St Paul's. Since Saxon times all five churches on this spot had been destroyed by fire. Wren designed the sixth as a sparkling symbol of London's rebirth, and he was there to witness its completion thirty-five years later. In the cathedral library you can see the huge and fabulously expensive oak model that the architect constructed to persuade Charles II to back his revolutionary concept. www.stpauls.co.uk.

Bell, George Walter, *The Great Fire of London in 1666* (London, Folio Society), 2003.

1678/9: Titus Oates and the Popish Plot

John Dryden's poem *Absalom and Achitophel* feverishly evokes the hysteria of the Popish Plot and the exclusion crisis. J. P. Kenyon recounts the story masterfully.

Kenyon, J. P., *The Popish Plot* (New York, Sterling), 2001.

1685: *Monmouth's Rebellion and the Bloody Assizes*
Christopher Lee starred as Judge Jeffreys in *The Bloody Judge* (1970), a film that has now acquired cult status. It is available on the DVD *The Christopher Lee Collection* by Blue Underground.

1688-9: *The Glorious Invasion*
Lord Macaulay virtually invented modern history, and his great five-volume work remains the classic study of the 1688/9 turning-point. Eveline Cruickshanks coldly dissects his Whig interpretation, but without destroying it.

Cruickshanks, Eveline, *The Glorious Revolution* (London, Macmillan), 2000.

Macaulay, T. B., *The History of England from the Accession of James II 1849-61*. The five volumes of Macaulay's classic are currently in print at three publishers (R.A. Kessinger Publishing, the University Press of the Pacific, and Indypublish.com) and also accessible online at various locations, including www.strecorsoc.org/macaulay/title.html#contents and www.gutenburg.net/etext/1468.

1687: *Isaac Newton and the Principles of the Universe*
There are modern apple trees in the orchard of Woolsthorpe Manor near Grantham in Lincolnshire, Isaac Newton's birthplace. Tel.: 01476 860338. The best account of the ferment of science and superstition surrounding the birth of the Royal Society is Lisa Jardine's sparkling study of Newton's great rival. The project to put all Newton's words on the web can be accessed on www.newtonproject.ic.ac.uk.

Jardine, Lisa, *The Curious Life of Robert Hooke* (London, HarperCollins), 2004.

ACKNOWLEDGEMENTS

The preceding source notes set out the books, articles and historical research on which I have relied in writing this book, but I owe a special debt to the historians who have given me personal help and advice — Dr Jacqueline Eales, Richard Eales, Dr Christopher Haigh, J. Patrick Hornbeck II, John McSween, Christopher Skidmore, Yvonne Ward and Patrick Wormald. I have also derived particular stimulation from my fellow committee members of the Society of Court Studies — Dr Andrew Barclay, Dr Anna Keay, our esteemed president Dr David Starkey, Dr Simon Thurley and Dr Mary Hollingsworth, who organises our seminars and the convivial evenings that follow. Thanks to Nabil Al-Khowaiter for his data on the Newton Project.

Nigel Rees once again helped me track down several fugitive quotations, and the National Archives joined the quest — but we are still looking for the first reliably recorded utterance of the words 'Glorious Revolution'. Nautical gratitude is due to the crew of The Matthew for their guidance in Bristol harbour, and to my mother for her hospitality while I was in Bristol and for her support at all times. Thanks, when it came to reference resources, to the librarians of the

British Library, the London Library, and the Westminster public library, as well as to the partners of the John Sandoe bookshop.

As with several previous projects, writing this book with the assistance of Moyra Ashford has made the process a pleasure. My wife Sandi — ever my best friend and critic — has been a particular support in helping to devise the illustrations so beautifully drawn by Fred van Deelen. In recent months I have been especially strengthened by the clarity offered by Prentis Hancock, Gregorio Kohon and Belinda Shand.

My thanks at Time Warner to Peter Cotton, David Young, Ursula Mackenzie, Sue Phillpott, David Atkinson, Jane Birkett and, in particular, to Roger Cazalet and the endlessly patient Viv Redman. Jonathan Pegg, my new agent at Curtis Brown, has worked hard on my behalf with Camilla Goslett and, more recently, with Shaheeda Sabir.

This volume, the second of three, is dedicated to my second child and only daughter Scarlett. She adds wonderful freshness to the ideas that I bounce off her in our transatlantic telephone calls, and I am deeply grateful for her unfailing emotional wisdom and support. She helped me think through the imagery of history as a kaleidoscope, and it is also thanks to her that I find myself revising the manuscript and writing these final words in the serene and stimulating atmosphere of the Esalen Institute at Big Sur, California.

Robert Lacey, August 2004

INDEX